# Thai & Chinese

**Publisher & Creative Director:** Nick Wells
**Senior Editor:** Cat Emslie
**Layouts:** Basil UK Ltd
**Production and Digital Design:** Chris Herbert
**Production Director:** Claire Walker
**With thanks to:** Gina Steer

This is a **FLAME TREE** Book

**FLAME TREE PUBLISHING**
Crabtree Hall, Crabtree Lane
Fulham, London SW6 6TY
United Kingdom
www.flametreepublishing.com

Flame Tree is part of The Foundry Creative Media Company Limited

First published 2007

Copyright © 2007 Flame Tree Publishing

09 11 10 08
3 5 7 9 10 8 6 4 2

ISBN: 978-1-84451-953-8

Printed in China

# Thai & Chinese

## Quick and Easy, Proven Recipes

FLAME TREE
PUBLISHING

# Contents

**Fresh Ingredients** 10

**Dry, Canned & Preserved Ingredients** 12

**Equipment & Techniques** 14

*Soups & Starters* 18

Clear Chicken & Mushroom Soup 20

Creamy Chicken & Tofu Soup 22

Wonton Noodle Soup 24

Thai Shellfish Soup 26

Moo Shi Pork 28

Crispy Pork Wontons 30

Mixed Satay Sticks 32

Sweetcorn Fritters 34

Thai Crab Cakes 36

Sesame Prawn Toasts 38

Sweet-&-Sour Battered Fish 40

Spicy Beef Pancakes 42

Lion's Head Pork Balls 44

Hot-&-Sour Squid 46

Spicy Prawns in Lettuce Cups 48

Cantonese Chicken Wings 50

Vegetable Thai Spring Rolls 52

Crispy Prawns with Chinese Dipping Sauce 54

Poached Fish Dumplings with Creamy Chilli Sauce 56

Thai Hot-&-Sour Prawn Soup 58

Sweetcorn & Crab Soup 60

Hot-&-Sour Soup 62

Chinese Leaf & Mushroom Soup 64

Laksa Malayan Rice Noodle Soup 66

Sesame Prawns 68

Barbecue Pork Steamed Buns 70

Chicken-filled Spring Rolls 72

Prawn Salad with Toasted Rice 74

Sticky Braised Spare Ribs 76

Soy-glazed Chicken Thighs 78

Shredded Duck in Lettuce Leaves 80

# Fish & Shellfish

**82**

| | |
|---|---|
| Steamed Monkfish with Chilli & Ginger | 84 |
| Red Prawn Curry with Jasmine-scented Rice | 86 |
| Thai Prawn & Rice Noodle Salad | 88 |
| Thai Curried Seafood | 90 |
| Fried Fish with Thai Chilli Dipping Sauce | 92 |
| Scallops & Prawns Braised in Lemon Grass | 94 |
| Fragrant Thai Swordfish with Peppers | 96 |
| Thai Coconut Crab Curry | 98 |
| Thai Marinated Prawns | 100 |
| Warm Lobster Salad with Hot Thai Dressing | 102 |
| Deep-fried Crab Wontons | 104 |

| | |
|---|---|
| Szechuan Chilli Prawns | 106 |
| Chinese Steamed Sea Bass with Black Beans | 108 |
| Sweet-&-Sour Fish | 110 |
| Fish Balls in Hot Yellow Bean Sauce | 112 |
| Steamed Whole Trout with Ginger & Spring Onion | 114 |
| Stir-fried Squid with Asparagus | 116 |
| Chinese Five Spice Marinated Salmon | 118 |
| Scallops with Black Bean Sauce | 120 |
| Stir-fried Tiger Prawns | 122 |
| Coconut Seafood | 124 |
| Lobster & Prawn Curry | 126 |
| Prawn Fried Rice | 128 |
| Teriyaki Salmon | 130 |
| Oriental Spicy Scallops | 132 |
| Crispy Prawn Stir Fry | 134 |
| Spicy Cod Rice | 136 |
| Creamy Spicy Shellfish | 138 |
| Tempura | 140 |

# Meat

**142**

| | |
|---|---|
| Pork Fried Noodles | 144 |
| Hoisin Pork | 146 |
| Coconut Beef | 148 |
| Pork Meatballs with Vegetables | 150 |
| Spicy Pork | 152 |
| Pork with Tofu & Coconut | 154 |

| | |
|---|---|
| Pork with Spring Vegetables & Sweet Chilli Sauce | 194 |
| Beef with Paprika | 196 |
| Fried Rice with Chilli Beef | 198 |
| Shredded Beef in Hoisin Sauce | 200 |
| Beef Curry with Lemon & Arborio Rice | 202 |

## *Poultry* 204

| | |
|---|---|
| Duck in Black Bean Sauce | 206 |
| Chinese–glazed Poussin with Green & Black Rice | 208 |
| Braised Chicken with Aubergine | 210 |
| Stir–fried Duck with Cashews | 212 |
| Stir–fried Lemon Chicken | 214 |
| Turkey & Vegetable Stir Fry | 216 |
| Crispy Roast Duck Legs with Pancakes | 218 |
| Chinese Barbecue–style Quails with Aubergines | 220 |

| | |
|---|---|
| Chilli Beef | 156 |
| Pork with Black Bean Sauce | 158 |
| Pork Spring Rolls | 160 |
| Special Fried Rice | 162 |
| Beef & Baby Corn Stir Fry | 164 |
| Sweet–&–Sour Spareribs | 166 |
| Lamb with Stir–fried Vegetables | 168 |
| Szechuan Beef | 170 |
| Cashew & Pork Stir Fry | 172 |
| Barbecued Pork Fillet | 174 |
| Spicy Lamb & Peppers | 176 |
| Pork Cabbage Parcels | 178 |
| Crispy Pork with Tangy Sauce | 180 |
| Speedy Pork with Yellow Bean Sauce | 182 |
| Honey Pork with Rice Noodles & Cashews | 184 |
| Sweet–&–Sour Pork | 186 |
| Chilli Lamb | 188 |
| Pork in Peanut Sauce | 190 |
| Stir–fried Beef with Vermouth | 192 |

# Contents

Chinese Braised White Chicken with Three Sauces  222

Orange Roasted Whole Chicken  224

Baked Thai Chicken Wings  226

Seared Duck with Pickled Plums  228

Thai Stuffed Omelette  230

Red Chicken Curry  232

Green Turkey Curry  234

Thai Chicken with Chilli & Peanuts  236

Thai Stir-fried Spicy Turkey  238

Hot-&-Sour Duck  240

Thai Chicken Fried Rice  242

Chicken in Black Bean Sauce  244

Green Chicken Curry  246

Chicken Chow Mein  248

Chicken Satay Salad  250

Duck in Crispy Wonton Shells  252

Chicken & Baby Vegetable Stir Fry  254

Sweet-&-Sour Turkey  256

Thai Coconut Chicken  258

Noodles with Turkey & Mushrooms  260

Chicken & Cashew Nuts  262

Szechuan Turkey Noodles  264

Lime & Sesame Turkey  266

Hoisin Duck & Greens Stir Fry  268

Duck & Exotic Fruit Stir Fry  270

Teriyaki Duck with Plum Chutney  272

Steamed, Crispy, Citrus Chicken  274

## Rice & Noodles  276

Thai Spring Rolls with Noodles & Dipping Sauce  278

Singapore Noodles  280

Oriental Noodle & Peanut Salad with Coriander  282

Char Sui Pork & Noodle Salad  284

Thai Rice Cakes with Mango Salsa  286

Thai Fried Rice with Prawns & Chillies  288

Chicken with Noodles  290

Chinese Bean Sauce Noodles  292

Beef Noodle Soup  294

Chicken Noodle Soup  296

Crispy Noodle Salad  298

Thai Spicy Prawn & Lettuce Noodle Soup  300

Seafood Noodle Salad  302

Chinese Fried Rice  304

# Vegetables

**306**

Warm Noodle Salad with Sesame & Peanut Dressing 308
Chinese Egg Fried Rice 310
Vegetable Tempura 312
Thai-style Cauliflower & Potato Curry 314
Cooked Vegetable Salad with Satay Sauce 316
Mixed Vegetables Stir Fry 318
Thai Stuffed Eggs with Spinach & Sesame Seeds 320
Savoury Wontons 322
Corn Fritters with Hot & Spicy Relish 324
Chinese Leaves with Sweet-&-Sour Sauce 326
Bean & Cashew Stir Fry 328
Fried Rice with Bamboo Shoots & Ginger 330
Thai Curry with Tofu 332
Chinese Omelette 334
Crispy Pancake Rolls 336
Vegetables in Coconut Milk with Rice Noodles 338

# Entertaining & Desserts

**340**

Sweet-&-Sour Shredded Beef 342
Kung-pao Lamb 344
Chicken & Lamb Satay 346
Szechuan Sesame Chicken 348
Turkey with Oriental Mushrooms 350
Crispy Aromatic Duck 352
Honey-glazed Duck in Kumquat Sauce 354
Dim Sum Pork Parcels 356
Pork with Tofu 358
Thai Green Fragrant Mussels 360
Ginger Lobster 362
Sour-&-Spicy Prawn Soup 364
Royal Fried Rice 366
Stir-fried Greens 368
Prawn Special Fried Rice 370
Coconut Sorbet with Mango Sauce 372
Rose-water Doughballs with Yogurt Sauce 374
Chocolate & Lemon Grass Mousse 376
Coconut Rice Served with Stewed Ginger Fruits 378
Hot Cherry Fritters 380

Index 382

# Fresh Ingredients

Most Oriental ingredients are now available in ordinary supermarkets and a few of the more unusual ones in Asian or Chinese groceries and markets. Here are just a few...

**BAMBOO SHOOTS** Bamboo shoots are young, creamy-coloured shoots of edible bamboo plants. They add a crunchy texture and clean, mild flavour to many dishes and are available vacuum-packed or canned in most supermarkets. Once opened, canned beansprouts will keep for up to five days in a container, refrigerated, with the water changed daily.

**BLACK BEANS** These small, black soya beans may also be known as salted black beans, as they have been fermented

with salt and spices. Sold loose in Chinese groceries, but also available canned, they have a rich flavour and are often used with ginger and garlic with which they have a particular affinity.

**BEANSPROUTS** These are the shoots of the mung bean and are readily available in most supermarkets. They add a wonderfully crisp texture when added to stir-fries and take only a minute or two to cook. Ideally, the brown root should be removed from each sprout and discarded in order to improve the appearance of the dish.

**BOK CHOI** Also known as pak choi, the most common variety has long, slightly ridged white stems like celery and large, oval thick dark green leaves. It has a mild, fresh, slightly peppery taste and needs very little cooking. The smaller ones are more tender. Store in the bottom of the refrigerator.

**CHINESE LEAVES** Also known as Chinese cabbage, Chinese leaves look like a large, tightly packed lettuce with crinkly, pale green leaves. It adds a crunchy texture to stir-fries.

**CHINESE MUSTARD CABBAGE** Also known as gaai choi, these mustard plants are similar in appearance to cabbages. The whole leaf is eaten, usually shredded into soups and stir-fries to which they add a fresh astringent flavour.

**CHINESE CELERY** Unlike the Western variety, Chinese celery stalks are thin, hollow and very crisp and range from pure white to dark green. Used as both a herb and a vegetable, it is often stir-fried or used in soups and braised dishes.

**CORIANDER** Fresh coriander is the most popular fresh herb used in Thai cooking. It has an appearance similar to flat-leaf parsley, but has a pungent, slightly citrus flavour. Leaves, stems and roots are all used, so buy in big fresh bunches if possible.

**CHILLIES** There are many different kinds of chillies and generally, the smaller they are the more fierce the heat. Red chillies are generally milder than green ones because they sweeten as they become riper. The tiny, slender tapering red or green Thai chillies are very hot and pungent. To moderate the heat, scrape out and discard the seeds.

**GALANGAL** This is called laos or ka in Thailand. It is similar to ginger, but the skin is pinkish and the flavour more complex and mellow.

**GINGER** Fresh root ginger has a pungent, spicy, fresh taste. It is usually peeled, then finely chopped or grated. Fresh ginger is infinitely preferable to the powdered variety, which loses its flavour rapidly. It should feel firm when you buy it and should be used within a week. It can be grated from frozen.

**KAFFIR LIME LEAVES** Dark green, smooth, glossy leaves, these come from the kaffir lime tree and are highly sought after for Thai cooking. They add a distinctive citrus flavour to curries, soups and sauces. Buy them from larger supermarkets and Oriental grocery shops and keep them in a sealed polythene bag in the freezer. Lime zest can be used as an alternative.

**LEMON GRASS** These look a bit like spring onions, but are much tougher. The stems should be bashed to release the lemony flavour during cooking, then removed before serving.

**TAMARIND** This adds an essential sour taste to many dishes. It is extracted from the pods as a sticky brown pulp, which is soaked to make tamarind water.

**TOFU** Tofu or bean curd has been used as an ingredient in Thai and Chinese cooking for over 1,000 years. Made from yellow soya beans, which are soaked, ground and briefly cooked, tofu is very rich in protein and low in calories. Because of its bland taste it is ideal cooked with stronger flavourings. It is usually available in two types: a soft variety known as silken tofu that can be used for soups and desserts, and a firm, solid white block, which can be cubed or sliced and included in stir-frying and braising. Cut into the required size with care and do not stir too much when cooking; it simply needs to be heated through.

**WATER CHESTNUTS** These are bulbs of an Asian water plant that look like and are a similar size to chestnuts. When peeled, the inner flesh is very crisp. Some Oriental grocers sell them fresh, although canned, either whole or sliced, are almost as good.

# Dry, Canned & Preserved Ingredients

**STAR ANISE** This is an eight-pointed, star-shaped pod with a strong aniseed flavour. It is added whole to many Chinese dishes, but is usually removed before serving. It is also a vital ingredient in Chinese five spice powder.

**CORIANDER** Ground coriander is made from coriander seeds and has an almost sweet, spicy, fresh flavour. Buy it ready ground or toast whole seeds in the oven and grind them yourself.

**CASHEW NUTS** These milky-flavoured nuts with a crunchy texture, are often used whole or chopped in Chinese cooking, particularly as an ingredient in chicken dishes.

**CHILLIES** Dried red chillies are used throughout Thailand and in much of China. The drying process concentrates the flavour, making them more fiery. If stored in a sealed container, they will keep almost indefinitely. Chilli oil is made from crushed dried chillies or whole fresh chillies and is used as both a seasoning and a dipping condiment. Chilli powder is made from dried red chillies and is usually mixed with other spices and seasonings.

**COCONUT MILK** Rich, creamy coconut milk is extracted from the white flesh of the nut. It can be bought in cans or made by adding boiling water to a sachet of coconut powder. Sometimes an opaque, white cream rises to the top of canned coconut milk and solidifies. You should shake the can before opening. If the milk is stored in an airtight container in the refrigerator it will last for up to three days, however, it does not freeze well. Occasionally, freshly made coconut milk may be bought from Oriental groceries. It is often used in Thai cooking, especially in curries and may also be used in desserts. Creamed coconut is not a substitute for coconut milk and is usually added at the end of cooking, to thicken a sauce, or to add coconut flavour to a finished dish.

**MUSHROOMS** Many sorts of dried mushrooms are used in Thai and Chinese cooking. Cloud ear (black fungus) mushrooms need soaking in warm water for about 20 minutes before use. They have a subtle, mild flavour and are highly regarded for their colour and gelatinous texture. Dried shiitake mushrooms have a very strong flavour and are used in small quantities.

**RICE** Glutinous, or 'sticky', rice is a short-grain variety often used in desserts. Thai Jasmine rice is a long-grain rice with an aromatic and subtle flavour.

**RICE VINEGARS AND WINE** There are several varieties of rice vinegar: white vinegar is clear and mild; red vinegar is slightly sweet and quite salty and is often used as a dipping sauce; black vinegar is very rich, yet mild and sweet vinegar is very thick, dark-coloured and flavoured with star anise. Rice Wine is used in Chinese cooking in both marinades and sauces. It is made from glutinous rice and has a rich, mellow taste. Do not confuse rice wine with the very different, Japanese, sake. Pale dry sherry is a good substitute for rice wine.

**GROUNDNUT OIL** Also known as peanut oil, this has a mild, nutty flavour. Because it can be heated to high temperatures, it is ideal for both stir-frying and deep-frying.

**SESAME OIL** This is a thick, dark-golden to brown aromatic oil made from sesame seeds. It is rarely used in frying, as it has a low smoke-point, but when it is, it should be combined with another oil. It is often added to a finished dish in small amounts.

**HOISIN SAUCE** This is a thick, dark brownish-red sauce, which is sweet, tangy and spicy. Made from soya beans, salt, flour, sugar, vinegar, chilli, garlic and sesame oil, it may be used as a dip, in 'red-cooking' and as a baste for roasted meats.

**NAM PLA FISH SAUCE** This is a golden brown, thin sauce with a salty flavour and is made from salted and fermented fresh fish, usually anchovies. It is used in Thai cooking in much the same way as soy sauce is used in Chinese cooking. The fishy aroma is almost unpleasant when the bottle is opened, but this mellows when mixed with other ingredients, adding a unique Thai flavour.

**OYSTER SAUCE** This is a thick, brown sauce made from oysters cooked in soy sauce. It has a wonderfully rich, but not fishy flavour, as this disappears during processing. Often used as a condiment, it is also one of the most used ingredients in southern Chinese cuisine.

**SOY SAUCE** Both light and dark soy sauce feature frequently in Chinese and Thai cooking. It is made from a mixture of soya beans, flour and water that are fermented together and allowed to age. The resulting liquid which is then distilled is soy sauce. Light soy sauce has a lighter colour and is more salty than the dark variety. It is often labelled as 'superior soy'. Dark soy sauce is aged for longer and the colour is almost black. Its flavour is stronger and is slightly thicker than light soy sauce. Confusingly, this is labelled in Thai and Chinese food shops as 'Soy Superior sauce'.

# Equipment & Techniques

## Equipment

### WOK

The most useful piece of equipment is, of course, the wok. It is much easier to use than a frying pan because of its depth, making it easier to toss the food around quickly without spilling it. A wok also requires a lot less oil for deep-frying than a deep-fat fryer, although more care is required in terms of safety. Also, the shape of the wok allows heat to spread more evenly, ensuring that the food cooks much more quickly.

There are a number of shapes of wok available. The Cantonese wok has short handles on each side. This type of wok is best for steaming and deep-frying because it is easier

to move when full of liquid. The Pau wok has a single handle and is better for stir-frying, allowing you to manoeuvre the pan with one hand while stirring the food with the other one.

Woks can also have rounded or slightly flattened bases. Round-bottomed woks are really only suitable for use on gas hobs. Flattened-bottomed woks can be used on gas and electric hobs but are better for deep-frying than stir-frying.

When choosing a wok, look for a large one simply because it is easier to cook a small amount in a large wok than a large amount in a small one. Choose a wok that is heavy and made of carbon steel, rather than stainless steel or aluminium, which tend to scorch. Non-stick woks are also available but these cannot be seasoned or used over very high temperatures, both of which are essential for flavour in stir-frying. Electric woks are also available, but these cannot be heated sufficiently hot enough and tend to have very shallow sides. They also lack the manoeuvrability of a free-standing wok.

If you buy a carbon-steel wok, it will need to be seasoned before use. First, scrub well using a cream cleanser or another abrasive to remove the machine oil with which it will probably have been coated to prevent rusting. Dry it well and then place it over a low heat. Add a little cooking oil and rub this all over the cooking surface with wadded kitchen paper. Continue heating over a low heat for 10–15 minutes, then wipe well with more kitchen paper – the paper will blacken. Repeat this process of coating, heating and wiping until the kitchen paper comes away clean. With continued use, the wok will darken further.

Do not scrub a seasoned wok with soap and water. Wash in hot, plain water using a brush or non-stick scrubber. Dry thoroughly with kitchen paper and place over a low heat until completely dry. Rub with a few drops of cooking oil to prevent rusting. If a little rust does appear, scrub off with cream cleanser or another abrasive and repeat the seasoning process.

## ACCESSORIES

If your hob will not support a free-standing wok, Oriental stores sell metal rings or frames, called wok stands, that stabilize round-bottomed woks. They are available in two designs: one is a solid ring punched with ventilation holes and the other is a circular wire frame. Only use the wire frame stand if you have a gas hob as the other stand will not allow sufficient ventilation.

You may also find it useful to have a lid for your wok. Wok lids are dome-like in shape, are usually made from aluminium and are very inexpensive. Any dome-shaped pan lid that fits snugly over the wok will suffice. Alternatively, use kitchen foil.

A long-handled spatula is also an important piece of equipment. Special spatulas with rounded ends are readily available and make stirring and tossing food in the wok much easier. A long-handled spoon can be used instead.

For steaming, it may be worth investing in a bamboo steamer. They are both attractive and effective. They come in a variety of sizes and stack together with the uppermost basket having a lid. Fill the steamer with food, placing the food needing the longest cooking time in the bottom basket and the more delicate foods in the top basket. Stand the steamer on a wooden or metal rack or trivet in a steady wok of boiling water. Cover tightly and leave to cook.

Chinese cooks would not be without a cleaver. It differs from a meat cleaver in that it has a finer, much sharper blade and is used for all kinds of cutting, from shredding to chopping up bones. Several types of Chinese cleavers are available including a light-weight, narrow-bladed cleaver for cutting delicate foods such as vegetables, a medium-weight model for general use and a heavy cleaver for heavy-duty chopping.

Another useful piece of equipment if you plan to do a lot of cooking in the wok is an electric rice cooker. It will cook rice perfectly and keep it warm, sometimes up to several hours. It also has the advantage of freeing-up cooker space.

Chopsticks are used in Chinese and Japanese cookery not just for eating but for stirring, beating and whipping. They are available in wood and plastic and can be bought in Oriental grocers and department stores. Chinese chopsticks are larger with blunted ends, while Japanese chopsticks tend to be smaller with pointed ends. To use chopsticks, put one chopstick into the crook of your preferred hand, between your thumb and first finger, holding the chopstick about two-thirds of the way up from the thinner end. Let it rest on your third finger. Put the second chopstick between your thumb and fore-finger so that its tip is level with the chopstick below. Keep the lower chopstick steady and move the top one to pick up food.

# Techniques

## CUTTING TECHNIQUES

**CHOPPING** This is the simplest technique and refers to simply cutting food through. Place the food on a firm surface, then using a straight, sharp, downward motion, chop through, hitting down with the blade, then finish off the blow with the flat of your other hand on the top edge of the knife or cleaver. A heavy cleaver or knife is best for these tasks.

**SLICING** This is the conventional method of laying the food firmly on a chopping board and slicing straight down to cut the food into thin slices. Meat is always sliced across the grain to break up the fibres and to make it more tender when cooked. If you use a cleaver, hold the cleaver with your index finger over the far side of the top of the cleaver and your thumb on the side nearest to you and guide the cutting edge firmly through

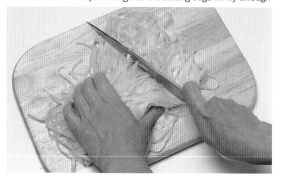

the food. With your other hand, hold the food and make sure when cutting that you turn your fingers under for safety.

**DIAGONAL SLICING** This is particularly useful for vegetables as it exposes more surface area to the heat of the wok and also makes the food look much more interesting. Simply angle the knife or cleaver against the food and slice.

**HORIZONTAL OR FLAT SLICING** This is a technique for slicing whole foods thinly, while retaining the overall shape. A cleaver is particularly useful for this technique. Hold the knife or cleaver with the blade parallel to the chopping board. Place your free hand on top of the food to be sliced. Using a gentle slicing motion, slice side-ways into the food and right the way through, taking care to keep your upper hand out of the way.

**SHREDDING** This is cutting food into fine, matchstick shreds. First cut the food into slices, then stack the slices and cut again, lengthways, into fine shreds. It can be easier to cut meat and fish if you put them in the freezer for 20–30 minutes beforehand.

**DICING** This is a simple technique of cutting food into small cubes. First cut the food into slices as for shredding. Stack the slices and slice again lengthways into sticks, again as you would for shredding. Turn again and cut crossways into cubes.

**MINCING** This is a very fine chopping technique. First slice the food and then chop it rapidly – it will spread out over the chopping area. Gather it into a pile and continue chopping and regathering until the food is chopped as finely as needed.

# COOKING TECHNIQUES

**STIR-FRYING** This is the most famous of wok techniques and is possibly the most tricky because it involves a lot of preparation as well as a good source of heat. Its advantage is that stir-fried foods can be cooked very quickly in very little oil so that they retain their colour, flavour and texture. It is very important that stir-fried foods are not greasy or overcooked.

**SHALLOW-FRYING** This is similar to sautéing as it involves more oil than stir-frying, but less than deep-frying. Food is fried first on one side and then on the other. A frying pan is preferable for shallow-frying rather than a wok.

**DEEP-FRYING** This is another very important technique in Far Eastern cookery. Woks are very useful for deep-frying as they use far less oil than conventional deep-fat fryers. Ensure that the wok sits securely on the hob. Carefully add the oil, ensuring that the wok is no more than half full. Heat up slowly to the required temperature. To test for temperature, either use a thermometer made for the purpose or add a small cube of crustless bread and time how long it takes to brown. Generally, if the bread browns in 30 seconds, the oil is at the correct temperature. Allow the oil to return to the correct temperature between batches of food and do not overfill the wok. Do not leave the wok unsupervised on the stove.

It is also important that food to be deep-fried is dry. Lift food from a marinade and blot thoroughly on kitchen paper. If using batter, allow any excess to drip off before adding to the oil. The oil can be reused for the same type of food up to 3 times.

**BLANCHING** This method involves cooking food in boiling water or moderately hot oil for a few minutes so that it is partly cooked, which speeds up the cooking process later on, so that other elements of the dish do not overcook.

**BRAISING** This is a method often applied to tougher cuts of meat that need long, slow cooking times to remain moist. The food is usually browned and then cooked in stock or liquid to which other flavourings are also added. The mixture is brought up to simmering point and then cooked gently until tender.

**POACHING** This is a method of cooking meat or fish in simmering liquid until nearly cooked so that it can be added to soup or combined with a sauce to finish the cooking.

**STEAMING** Steamed foods are cooked on a gentle, moist heat. Steaming adds no fat to the food being cooked and is particularly suited to vegetables and fish. See page 15 for using a bamboo steamer. You can also arrange the food on a plate on top of a trivet in a wok filled with 5 cm/2 inches of boiling water and then cover the wok tightly with a lid.

# Soups & Starters

# Clear Chicken & Mushroom Soup

**SERVES 4**

2 large chicken legs, about 450 g/1 lb total weight
1 tbsp groundnut oil
1 tsp sesame oil
1 onion, peeled and very thinly sliced
2.5 cm/1 inch piece root ginger, peeled and very finely chopped
1.1 litres/2 pints clear chicken stock
1 lemon grass stalk, bruised
50 g/2 oz long-grain rice
75 g/3 oz button mushrooms, wiped and finely sliced
4 spring onions, trimmed, cut into 5 cm/2 inch pieces and shredded
1 tbsp dark soy sauce
4 tbsp dry sherry
salt and freshly ground black pepper

Skin the chicken legs and remove any fat. Cut each in half to make 2 thigh and 2 drumstick portions and reserve. Heat the groundnut and sesame oils in a large saucepan. Add the sliced onion and cook gently for 10 minutes, or until soft but not beginning to colour.

Add the chopped ginger to the saucepan and cook for about 30 seconds, stirring all the time to prevent it sticking, then pour in the stock. Add the chicken pieces and the lemon grass, cover and simmer gently for 15 minutes. Stir in the rice and cook for a further 15 minutes or until the chicken is cooked.

Remove the chicken from the saucepan and leave until cool enough to handle. Finely shred the flesh, then return to the saucepan with the mushrooms, spring onions, soy sauce and sherry. Simmer for 5 minutes, or until the rice and mushrooms are tender. Remove the lemon grass.

Season the soup to taste with salt and pepper. Ladle into warmed serving bowls, making sure each has an equal amount of shredded chicken and vegetables and serve immediately.

*Try this:* FOR AN ALTERNATIVE: 64   FOR A MORE SUBSTANTIAL OPTION: 296

# Creamy Chicken & Tofu Soup

**SERVES 4-6**

225 g/8 oz firm tofu, drained
3 tbsp groundnut oil
1 garlic clove, peeled
   and crushed
2.5 cm/1 inch piece root
   ginger, peeled and
   finely chopped
2.5 cm/1 inch piece fresh
   galangal, peeled and

finely sliced (if available)
1 lemon grass stalk, bruised
¼ tsp ground turmeric
600 ml/1 pint chicken stock
600 ml/1 pint coconut milk
225 g/8 oz cauliflower, cut
   into tiny florets
1 medium carrot, peeled and
   cut into thin matchsticks

125 g/4 oz green beans,
   trimmed and cut in half
75 g/3 oz thin egg noodles
225 g/8 oz cooked chicken,
   shredded
salt and freshly ground
   black pepper

Cut the tofu into 1 cm/½ inch cubes, then pat dry on absorbent kitchen paper.

Heat 1 tablespoon of the oil in a nonstick frying pan. Fry the tofu in 2 batches for 3–4 minutes or until golden brown. Remove, drain on absorbent kitchen paper and reserve.

Heat the remaining oil in a large saucepan. Add the garlic, ginger, galangal and lemon grass and cook for about 30 seconds. Stir in the turmeric, then pour in the stock and coconut milk and bring to the boil. Reduce the heat to a gentle simmer, add the cauliflower and carrots and simmer for 10 minutes. Add the green beans and simmer for a further 5 minutes.

Meanwhile, bring a large saucepan of lightly salted water to the boil. Add the noodles, turn off the heat, cover and leave to cook or cook according to the packet instructions.

Remove the lemon grass from the soup. Drain the noodles and stir into the soup with the chicken and browned tofu. Season to taste with salt and pepper, then simmer gently for 2–3 minutes or until heated through. Serve immediately in warmed soup bowls.

*Try this:* FOR AN ALTERNATIVE: 20  FOR A MORE SUBSTANTIAL OPTION: 296

# Wonton Noodle Soup

**SERVES 4**

4 shiitake mushrooms,
  wiped
125 g/4 oz raw prawns,
  peeled and finely chopped
125 g/4 oz pork mince
4 water chestnuts,
  finely chopped

4 spring onions, trimmed
  and finely sliced
1 medium egg white
salt and freshly ground
  black pepper
1½ tsp cornflour
1 packet fresh wonton

  wrappers
1.1 litres/2 pints chicken stock
2 cm/¾ inch piece root
  ginger, peeled and sliced
75 g/3 oz thin egg noodles
125 g/4 oz pak choi,
  shredded

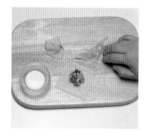

Place the mushrooms in a bowl, cover with warm water and leave to soak for 1 hour. Drain, remove and discard the stalks and finely chop the mushrooms. Return to the bowl with the prawns, pork, water chestnuts, 2 of the spring onions and egg white. Season to taste with salt and pepper. Mix well.

Mix the cornflour with 1 tablespoon of cold water to make a paste. Place a wonton wrapper on a board and brush the edges with the paste. Drop a little less than 1 teaspoon of the pork mixture in the centre then fold in half to make a triangle, pressing the edges together. Bring the 2 outer corners together, fixing together with a little more paste. Continue until all the pork mixture is used up; you should have 16–20 wontons.

Pour the stock into a large wide saucepan, add the ginger slices and bring to the boil. Add the wontons and simmer for about 5 minutes. Add the noodles and cook for 1 minute. Stir in the pak choi and cook for a further 2 minutes, or until the noodles and pak choi are tender and the wontons have floated to the surface and are cooked through.

Ladle the soup into warmed bowls, discarding the ginger. Sprinkle with the remaining sliced spring onion and serve immediately.

*Try this:* FOR AN ALTERNATIVE: 66  FOR A MORE SUBSTANTIAL OPTION: 294

# Thai Shellfish Soup

**SERVES 4-6**

350 g/12 oz raw prawns
350 g/12 oz firm white fish,
  such as monkfish, cod
  or haddock
175 g/6 oz small squid rings
1 tbsp lime juice

450 g/1 lb live mussels
400 ml/15 fl oz coconut milk
1 tbsp groundnut oil
2 tbsp Thai red curry paste
1 lemon grass stalk, bruised
3 kaffir lime leaves,

  finely shredded
2 tbsp Thai fish sauce
salt and freshly ground
  black pepper
fresh coriander leaves,
  to garnish

Peel the prawns. Using a sharp knife, remove the black vein along the back of the prawns. Pat dry with absorbent kitchen paper and reserve. Skin the fish, pat dry and cut into 2.5 cm/1 inch chunks. Place in a bowl with the prawns and the squid rings. Sprinkle with the lime juice and reserve.

Scrub the mussels, removing their beards and any barnacles. Discard any mussels that are open, damaged or that do not close when tapped. Place in a large saucepan and add 150 ml/¼ pint of coconut milk. Cover, bring to the boil, then simmer for 5 minutes, or until the mussels open, shaking the saucepan occasionally. Lift out the mussels, discarding any unopened ones, strain the liquid through a muslin-lined sieve and reserve.

Rinse and dry the saucepan. Heat the groundnut oil, add the curry paste and cook for 1 minute, stirring all the time. Add the lemon grass, lime leaves, fish sauce and pour in both the strained and the remaining coconut milk. Bring the contents of the saucepan to a very gentle simmer.

Add the fish mixture to the saucepan and simmer for 2–3 minutes or until just cooked. Stir in the mussels, with or without their shells as preferrred. Season to taste with salt and pepper, then garnish with coriander leaves. Ladle into warmed bowls and serve immediately.

# Moo Shi Pork

**SERVES 4**

175 g/6 oz pork fillet
2 tsp Chinese rice wine or
  dry sherry
2 tbsp light soy sauce
1 tsp cornflour
25 g/1 oz dried golden
  needles, soaked
  and drained

2 tbsp groundnut oil
3 medium eggs,
  lightly beaten
1 tsp freshly grated
  root ginger
3 spring onions, trimmed
  and thinly sliced
150 g/5 oz bamboo shoots,

  cut into fine strips
salt and freshly ground
  black pepper
8 mandarin pancakes,
  steamed hoisin sauce
sprigs of fresh coriander,
  to garnish

Cut the pork across the grain into 1 cm/½ inch slices, then cut into thin strips. Place in a bowl with the Chinese rice wine or sherry, soy sauce and cornflour. Mix well and reserve. Trim off the tough ends of the golden needles, then cut in half and reserve.

Heat a wok or large frying pan, add 1 tablespoon of the groundnut oil and when hot, add the lightly beaten eggs, and cook for 1 minute, stirring all the time, until scrambled. Remove and reserve. Wipe the wok clean with absorbent kitchen paper.

Return the wok to the heat, add the remaining oil and when hot transfer the pork strips from the marinade mixture to the wok, shaking off as much marinade as possible. Stir-fry for 30 seconds, then add the ginger, spring onions and bamboo shoots and pour in the marinade. Stir-fry for 2–3 minutes or until cooked.

Return the scrambled eggs to the wok, season to taste with salt and pepper and stir for a few seconds until mixed well and heated through. Divide the mixture between the pancakes, drizzle each with 1 teaspoon of hoisin sauce and roll up. Garnish and serve immediately.

*Try this:* FOR AN ALTERNATIVE: 30  FOR A MORE SUBSTANTIAL OPTION: 146

# Crispy Pork Wontons

## SERVES 4

1 small onion, peeled and roughly chopped
2 garlic cloves, peeled and crushed
1 green chilli, deseeded and chopped
2.5 cm/1 inch piece fresh

root ginger, peeled and roughly chopped
450 g/1 lb lean pork mince
4 tbsp freshly chopped coriander
1 tsp Chinese five spice powder

salt and freshly ground black pepper
20 wonton wrappers
1 medium egg, lightly beaten
vegetable oil for deep-frying
chilli sauce, to serve

Place the onion, garlic, chilli and ginger in a food processor and blend until very finely chopped. Add the pork, coriander and Chinese five spice powder. Season to taste with salt and pepper, then blend again briefly to mix. Divide the mixture into 20 equal portions and with floured hands shape each into a walnut-sized ball.

Brush the edges of a wonton wrapper with beaten egg, place a pork ball in the centre, then bring the corners to the centre and pinch together to make a money bag. Repeat with the remaining pork balls and wrappers.

Pour sufficient oil into a heavy-based saucepan or deep-fat fryer so that it is one-third full and heat to 180°C/350°F. Deep-fry the wontons in 3 or 4 batches for 3–4 minutes, or until cooked through and golden and crisp. Drain on absorbent kitchen paper. Serve the crispy pork wontons immediately, allowing 5 per person, with some chilli sauce for dipping.

*Try this:* FOR AN ALTERNATIVE: 72  FOR A MORE SUBSTANTIAL OPTION: 322

# Mixed Satay Sticks

**SERVES 4**

12 large raw prawns
350 g/12 oz beef rump steak
1 tbsp lemon juice
1 garlic clove, peeled
 and crushed
salt
2 tsp soft dark brown sugar
1 tsp ground cumin

1 tsp ground coriander
¼ tsp ground turmeric
1 tbsp groundnut oil
fresh coriander leaves,
 to garnish

**For the spicy peanut sauce:**
1 shallot, peeled and very

 finely chopped
1 tsp demerara sugar
50 g/2 oz creamed
 coconut, chopped
pinch of chilli powder
1 tbsp dark soy sauce
125 g/4 oz crunchy
 peanut butter

Preheat the grill on high just before required. Soak 8 bamboo skewers in cold water for at least 30 minutes. Peel the prawns, leaving the tails on. Using a sharp knife, remove the black vein along the back of the prawns. Cut the beef into 1 cm/½ inch wide strips. Place the prawns and beef in separate bowls and sprinkle each with ½ tablespoon of the lemon juice.

Mix together the garlic, pinch of salt, sugar, cumin, coriander, turmeric and groundnut oil to make a paste. Lightly brush over the prawns and beef. Cover and place in the refrigerator to marinate for at least 30 minutes, but for longer if possible.

Meanwhile, make the sauce. Pour 125 ml/4 fl oz of water into a small saucepan, add the shallot and sugar and heat gently until the sugar has dissolved. Stir in the creamed coconut and chilli powder. When melted, remove from the heat and stir in the peanut butter. Leave to cool slightly, then spoon into a serving dish.

Thread 3 prawns on to each of 4 skewers and divide the sliced beef between the remaining skewers. Cook the skewers under the preheated grill for 4–5 minutes, turning occasionally. The prawns should be opaque and pink and the beef browned on the outside, but still pink in the centre. Transfer to warmed individual serving plates, garnish with a few fresh coriander leaves and serve immediately with the warm peanut sauce.

*Try this:* FOR AN ALTERNATIVE: 76  FOR A MORE SUBSTANTIAL OPTION: 342

# Sweetcorn Fritters

**SERVES 4**

4 tbsp groundnut oil
1 small onion, peeled and
    finely chopped
1 red chilli, deseeded and
    finely chopped
1 garlic clove, peeled
    and crushed

1 tsp ground coriander
325 g can sweetcorn
6 spring onions, trimmed
    and finely sliced
1 medium egg,
    lightly beaten
salt and freshly ground

black pepper
3 tbsp plain flour
1 tsp baking powder
spring onion curls,
    to garnish
Thai-style chutney,
    to serve

Heat 1 tablespoon of the groundnut oil in a frying pan, add the onion and cook gently for 7–8 minutes or until beginning to soften. Add the chilli, garlic and ground coriander and cook for 1 minute, stirring continuously. Remove from the heat.

Drain the sweetcorn and tip into a mixing bowl. Lightly mash with a potato masher to break down the corn a little. Add the cooked onion mixture to the bowl with the spring onions and beaten egg. Season to taste with salt and pepper, then stir to mix together. Sift the flour and baking powder over the mixture and stir in.

Heat 2 tablespoons of the groundnut oil in a large frying pan. Drop 4 or 5 heaped teaspoonfuls of the sweetcorn mixture into the pan, and using a fish slice or spatula, flatten each to make a 1 cm/½ inch thick fritter.

Fry the fritters for 3 minutes, or until golden brown on the underside, turn over and fry for a further 3 minutes, or until cooked through and crisp.

Remove the fritters from the pan and drain on absorbent kitchen paper. Keep warm while cooking the remaining fritters, adding a little more oil if needed. Garnish with spring onion curls and serve immediately with a Thai-style chutney.

*Try this:* FOR AN ALTERNATIVE: 36  FOR A MORE SUBSTANTIAL OPTION: 324

# Thai Crab Cakes

**SERVES 4**

225 g/8 oz white and brown
  crabmeat (about
  equivalent to the flesh
  of 2 medium crabs)
1 tsp ground coriander
¼ tsp chilli powder
¼ tsp ground turmeric
2 tsp lime juice

1 tsp soft light brown sugar
2.5 cm/1 inch piece fresh
  root ginger, peeled
  and grated
3 tbsp freshly chopped
  coriander
2 tsp finely chopped
  lemon grass

2 tbsp plain flour
2 medium eggs, separated
50 g/2 oz fresh white
  breadcrumbs
3 tbsp groundnut oil
lime wedges, to garnish
mixed salad leaves,
  to serve

Place the crabmeat in a bowl with the ground coriander, chilli, turmeric, lime juice, sugar, ginger, chopped coriander, lemon grass, flour and egg yolks. Mix together well.

Divide the mixture into 12 equal portions and form each into a small patty about 5 cm/2 inches across. Lightly whisk the egg whites and put into a dish. Place the breadcrumbs on a separate plate.

Dip each crab cake, first in the egg whites, then in the breadcrumbs, turning to coat both sides. Place on a plate, cover and chill in the refrigerator until ready to cook.

Heat the oil in a large frying pan. Add 6 crab cakes and cook for 3 minutes on each side, or until crisp and golden brown on the outside and cooked through. Remove, drain on absorbent kitchen paper and keep warm while cooking the remaining cakes. Arrange on plates, garnish with lime wedges and serve immediately with salad leaves.

*Try this:* FOR AN ALTERNATIVE: 40  FOR A MORE SUBSTANTIAL OPTION: 104

# Sesame Prawn Toasts

## SERVES 4

125 g/4 oz peeled
cooked prawns
1 tbsp cornflour
2 spring onions, peeled
and roughly chopped
2 tsp freshly grated

root ginger
2 tsp dark soy sauce
pinch of Chinese five-spice
powder (optional)
1 small egg, beaten
salt and freshly ground

black pepper
6 thin slices day-old
white bread
40 g/1½ oz sesame seeds
vegetable oil for deep-frying
chilli sauce, to serve

Place the prawns in a food processor or blender with the cornflour, spring onions, ginger, soy sauce and Chinese five spice powder, if using. Blend to a fairly smooth paste. Spoon into a bowl and stir in the beaten egg. Season to taste with salt and pepper.

Cut the crusts off the bread. Spread the prawn paste in an even layer on one side of each slice. Sprinkle over the sesame seeds and press down lightly.

Cut each slice diagonally into 4 triangles. Place on a board and chill in the refrigerator for 30 minutes.

Pour sufficient oil into a heavy-based saucepan or deep-fat fryer so that it is one-third full. Heat until it reaches a temperature of 180°C/350°F. Cook the toasts in batches of 5 or 6, carefully lowering them seeded-side down into the oil. Deep-fry for 2–3 minutes, or until lightly browned, then turn over and cook for 1 minute more. Using a slotted spoon, lift out the toasts and drain on absorbent kitchen paper. Keep warm while frying the remaining toasts. Arrange on a warmed platter and serve immediately with some chilli sauce for dipping.

 *Try this:* FOR AN ALTERNATIVE: 68  FOR A MORE SUBSTANTIAL OPTION: 100

# Sweet–&–Sour Battered Fish

**SERVES 4-6**

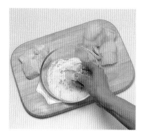

450 g/1 lb cod fillet, skinned
150 g/5 oz plain flour
salt and freshly ground
   black pepper
2 tbsp cornflour
2 tbsp arrowroot

vegetable oil for deep-frying

**For the sweet-&-sour sauce:**
4 tbsp orange juice
2 tbsp white wine vinegar
2 tbsp dry sherry

1 tbsp dark soy sauce
1 tbsp soft light brown sugar
2 tsp tomato purée
1 red pepper, deseeded
   and diced
2 tsp cornflour

Cut the fish into pieces about 5cm x 2.5cm/2 x 1 inch. Place 4 tablespoons of the flour in a small bowl, season with salt and pepper to taste, then add the fish strips a few at a time and toss until coated.

Sift the remaining flour into a bowl with a pinch of salt, the cornflour and arrowroot. Gradually whisk in 300 ml/½ pint iced water to make a smooth, thin batter.

Heat the oil in a wok or deep-fat fryer to 190°C/375°F. Working in batches, dip the fish strips in the batter and deep-fry them for 3–5 minutes, or until crisp. Using a slotted spoon, remove the strips and drain on absorbent kitchen paper.

Meanwhile, make the sauce. Place 3 tablespoons of the orange juice, the vinegar, sherry, soy sauce, sugar, tomato purée and red pepper in a small saucepan. Bring to the boil, lower the heat and simmer for 3 minutes.

Blend the cornflour with the remaining orange juice, stir into the sauce and simmer, stirring, for 1 minute or until thickened. Arrange the fish on a warmed platter or individual plates. Drizzle a little of the sauce over and serve immediately with the remaining sauce.

*Try this:* FOR AN ALTERNATIVE: 68  FOR A MORE SUBSTANTIAL OPTION: 110

# Spicy Beef Pancakes

**SERVES 4**

50 g/2 oz plain flour
pinch of salt
½ tsp Chinese five
   spice powder
1 large egg yolk
150 ml/¼ pint milk
4 tsp sunflower oil
slices of spring onion,
   to garnish

**For the spicy beef filling:**
1 tbsp sesame oil
4 spring onions, sliced
1 cm/½ inch piece fresh root
   ginger, peeled and grated
1 garlic clove, peeled
   and crushed
300 g/11 oz sirloin steak,
   trimmed and cut into strips

1 red chilli, deseeded and
   finely chopped
1 tsp sherry vinegar
1 tsp soft dark brown sugar
1 tbsp dark soy sauce

Sift the flour, salt and Chinese five spice powder into a bowl and make a well in the centre. Add the egg yolk and a little of the milk. Gradually beat in, drawing in the flour to make a smooth batter. Whisk in the rest of the milk. Heat 1 teaspoon of the sunflower oil in a small heavy-based frying pan. Pour in just enough batter to thinly coat the base of the pan. Cook over a medium heat for 1 minute, or until the underside of the pancake is golden brown.

Turn or toss the pancake and cook for 1 minute, or until the other side of the pancake is golden brown. Make 7 more pancakes with the remaining batter. Stack them on a warmed plate as you make them, with greaseproof paper between each pancake. Cover with tinfoil and keep warm in a low oven.

Make the filling. Heat a wok or large frying pan, add the sesame oil and when hot, add the spring onions, ginger and garlic and stir-fry for 1 minute. Add the beef strips, stir-fry for 3–4 minutes, then stir in the chilli, vinegar, sugar and soy sauce. Cook for 1 minute, then remove from the heat. Spoon one-eighth of the filling over one half of each pancake. Fold the pancakes in half, then fold in half again. Garnish with a few slices of spring onion and serve immediately.

*Try this:* FOR AN ALTERNATIVE: 30  FOR A MORE SUBSTANTIAL OPTION: 156

# Lion's Head Pork Balls

**SERVES 4**

75 g/3 oz glutinous rice
450 g/1 lb lean pork mince
2 garlic cloves, peeled
  and crushed
1 tbsp cornflour
½ tsp Chinese five
  spice powder
2 tsp dark soy sauce
1 tbsp Chinese rice wine

or dry sherry
2 tbsp freshly chopped
  coriander
salt and freshly ground
  black pepper

**For the sweet chilli
  dipping sauce:**
2 tsp caster sugar

1 tbsp sherry vinegar
1 tbsp light soy sauce
1 shallot, peeled and
  very finely chopped
1 small red chilli, deseeded
  and finely chopped
2 tsp sesame oil

Place the rice in a bowl and pour over plenty of cold water. Cover and soak for 2 hours. Tip into a sieve and drain well.

Place the pork, garlic, cornflour, Chinese five spice powder, soy sauce, Chinese rice wine or sherry and coriander in a bowl. Season to taste with salt and pepper and mix together.

With slightly wet hands, shape the pork mixture into 20 walnut-sized balls, then roll in the rice to coat. Place the balls slightly apart in a steamer or a colander set over a saucepan of boiling water, cover and steam for 20 minutes, or until cooked through.

Meanwhile, make the dipping sauce. Stir together the sugar, vinegar and soy sauce until the sugar dissolves. Add the shallot, chilli and sesame oil and whisk together with a fork. Transfer to a small serving bowl, cover and leave to stand for at least 10 minutes before serving.

Remove the pork balls from the steamer and arrange them on a warmed serving platter. Serve immediately with the sweet chilli dipping sauce.

*Try this:* FOR AN ALTERNATIVE: 70  FOR A MORE SUBSTANTIAL OPTION: 152

# Hot-&-Sour Squid

**SERVES 4**

8 baby squid, cleaned
2 tbsp dark soy sauce
2 tbsp hoisin sauce
1 tbsp lime juice
2 tbsp dry sherry
1 tbsp clear honey

2.5 cm/1 inch piece fresh
   root ginger, peeled and
   finely chopped
1 red chilli, deseeded
   and finely chopped
1 green chilli, deseeded and

   finely chopped
1 tsp cornflour
salt and freshly ground
   black pepper
vegetable oil for deep-frying
lime wedges, to garnish

Slice open the body of each squid lengthways, open out and place on a chopping board with the inside uppermost. Using a sharp knife, score lightly in a criss-cross pattern. Cut each one into 4 pieces. Trim the tentacles.

Place the soy and hoisin sauces with the lime juice, sherry, honey, ginger, chillies and cornflour in a bowl. Season to taste with salt and pepper and mix together. Add the squid, stir well to coat, then cover and place in the refrigerator to marinate for 1 hour.

Tip the squid into a sieve over a small saucepan and strain off the marinade. Scrape any bits of chilli or ginger into the saucepan, as they would burn if fried.

Fill a deep-fat fryer one-third full with oil and heat to 180°C/350°F. Deep-fry the squid in batches for 2–3 minutes or until golden and crisp. Remove the squid and drain on absorbent kitchen paper. Keep warm.

Bring the marinade to the boil and let it bubble gently for a few seconds. Arrange the squid on a warmed serving dish and drizzle over the marinade. Garnish with lime wedges and serve immediately.

*Try this:* FOR AN ALTERNATIVE: 58 FOR A MORE SUBSTANTIAL OPTION: 344

# Spicy Prawns in Lettuce Cups

**SERVES 4**

1 lemon grass stalk
225 g/8 oz peeled
    cooked prawns
1 tsp finely grated lime zest
1 red bird's-eye chilli,
    deseeded and
    finely chopped
2.5 cm/1 inch piece fresh
    root ginger, peeled

and grated
2 Little Gem lettuces,
    divided into leaves
25 g/1 oz roasted
    peanuts, chopped
2 spring onions, trimmed
    and diagonally sliced
sprig of fresh coriander,
    to garnish

**For the coconut sauce:**
2 tbsp freshly grated
    or unsweetened
    shredded coconut
1 tbsp hoisin sauce
1 tbsp light soy sauce
1 tbsp Thai fish sauce
1 tbsp palm sugar or soft
    light brown sugar

Remove 3 or 4 of the tougher outer leaves of the lemon grass and reserve for another dish. Finely chop the remaining softer centre. Place 2 teaspoons of the chopped lemon grass in a bowl with the prawns, grated lime zest, chilli and ginger. Mix together to coat the prawns. Cover and place in the refrigerator to marinate while you make the coconut sauce.

For the sauce, place the grated coconut in a wok or nonstick frying pan and dry-fry for 2–3 minutes or until golden. Remove from the pan and reserve. Add the hoisin, soy and fish sauces to the pan with the sugar and 4 tablespoons of water. Simmer for 2–3 minutes, then remove from the heat. Leave to cool.

Pour the sauce over the prawns, add the toasted coconut and toss to mix together. Divide the prawn and coconut sauce mixture between the lettuce leaves and arrange on a platter.

Sprinkle over the chopped roasted peanuts and spring onions and garnish with a sprig of fresh coriander. Serve immediately.

*Try this:* FOR AN ALTERNATIVE: 74 FOR A MORE SUBSTANTIAL OPTION: 100

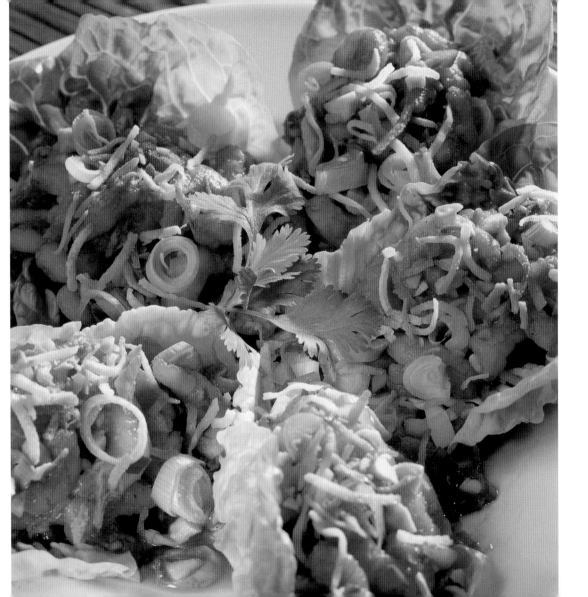

# Cantonese Chicken Wings

**SERVES 4**

3 tbsp hoisin sauce
2 tbsp dark soy sauce
1 tbsp sesame oil
1 garlic clove, peeled
　and crushed
2.5 cm/1 inch piece fresh
　root ginger, peeled

and grated
1 tbsp Chinese rice wine
　or dry sherry
2 tsp chilli bean sauce
2 tsp red or white
　wine vinegar
2 tbsp soft light brown sugar

900 g/2 lb large
　chicken wings
50 g/2 oz cashew
　nuts, chopped
2 spring onions, trimmed
　and finely chopped

Preheat the oven to 220°C/425°F/Gas Mark 7, 15 minutes before cooking. Place the hoisin sauce, soy sauce, sesame oil, garlic, ginger, Chinese rice wine or sherry, chilli bean sauce, vinegar and sugar in a small saucepan with 6 tablespoons of water. Bring to the boil, stirring occasionally, then simmer for about 30 seconds. Remove the glaze from the heat.

Place the chicken wings in a roasting tin in a single layer. Pour over the glaze and stir until the wings are coated thoroughly.

Cover the tin loosely with tinfoil, place in the preheated oven and roast for 25 minutes. Remove the tinfoil, baste the wings and cook for a further 5 minutes.

Reduce the oven temperature to 190°C/375°F/Gas Mark 5. Turn the wings over and sprinkle with the chopped cashew nuts and spring onions. Return to the oven and cook for 5 minutes, or until the nuts are lightly browned, the glaze is sticky and the wings are tender. Remove from the oven and leave to stand for 5 minutes before arranging on a warmed platter. Serve immediately with finger bowls and plenty of napkins.

*Try this:* FOR AN ALTERNATIVE: 78 FOR A MORE SUBSTANTIAL OPTION: 226

# Vegetable Thai Spring Rolls

**SERVES 4**

50 g/2 oz cellophane vermicelli
4 dried shiitake mushrooms
1 tbsp groundnut oil
2 medium carrots,
    peeled and cut into
    fine matchsticks
125 g/4 oz mangetout, cut
    lengthways into fine strips

3 spring onions, trimmed
    and chopped
125 g/4 oz canned
    bamboo shoots, cut
    into fine matchsticks
1 cm/½ inch piece fresh root
    ginger, peeled and grated
1 tbsp light soy sauce

1 medium egg, separated
salt and freshly ground
    black pepper
20 spring roll wrappers, each
    about 12.5 cm/5 inch square
vegetable oil for deep-frying
spring onion tassels,
    to garnish

Place the vermicelli in a bowl and pour over enough boiling water to cover. Leave to soak for 5 minutes or until softened, then drain. Cut into 7.5 cm/3 inch lengths. Soak the shiitake mushrooms in almost boiling water for 15 minutes, drain, discard the stalks and slice thinly.

Heat a wok or large frying pan, add the groundnut oil and when hot, add the carrots and stir-fry for 1 minute. Add the mangetout and spring onions and stir-fry for 2–3 minutes or until tender. Tip the vegetables into a bowl and leave to cool. Stir the vermicelli and shiitake mushrooms into the cooled vegetables with the bamboo shoots, ginger, soy sauce and egg yolk. Season to taste with salt and pepper and mix thoroughly.

Brush the edges of a spring roll wrapper with a little beaten egg white. Spoon 2 teaspoons of the vegetable filling on to the wrapper, in a 7.5 cm/3 inch log shape 2.5 cm/1 inch from one edge. Fold the wrapper edge over the filling, then fold in the right and left sides. Brush the folded edges with more egg white and roll up neatly. Place on an oiled baking sheet, seam-side down and make the rest of the spring rolls. Heat the oil in a heavy-based saucepan or deep-fat fryer to 180°C/350°F. Deep-fry the spring rolls, 6 at a time for 2–3 minutes, or until golden brown and crisp. Drain on absorbent kitchen paper and arrange on a warmed platter. Garnish with spring onion tassels and serve immediately.

*Try this* FOR AN ALTERNATIVE: 72 FOR A MORE SUBSTANTIAL OPTION: 278

# Crispy Prawns with Chinese Dipping Sauce

**SERVES 4**

450 g/1 lb medium-sized
    raw prawns, peeled
¼ tsp salt
6 tbsp groundnut oil
2 garlic cloves, peeled and
    finely chopped
2.5 cm/1 inch piece fresh

root ginger, peeled and
    finely chopped
1 green chilli, deseeded and
    finely chopped
4 stems fresh coriander,
    leaves and stems
    roughly chopped

**For the dipping sauce:**
3 tbsp dark soy sauce
3 tbsp rice wine vinegar
1 tbsp caster sugar
2 tbsp chilli oil
2 spring onions,
    finely shredded

Using a sharp knife, remove the black vein along the back of the prawns. Sprinkle the prawns with the salt and leave to stand for 15 minutes. Pat dry on absorbent kitchen paper.

Heat a wok or large frying pan, add the groundnut oil and when hot, add the prawns and stir-fry in 2 batches for about 1 minute, or until they turn pink and are almost cooked. Using a slotted spoon, remove the prawns and keep warm in a low oven.

Drain the oil from the wok, leaving 1 tablespoon. Add the garlic, ginger and chilli and cook for about 30 seconds. Add the coriander, return the prawns and stir-fry for 1–2 minutes, or until the prawns are cooked through and the garlic is golden. Turn into a warmed serving dish.

For the dipping sauce, using a fork, beat together the soy sauce, rice vinegar, caster sugar and chilli oil in a small bowl. Stir in the spring onions. Serve immediately with the hot prawns.

*Try this:* FOR AN ALTERNATIVE: 68 FOR A MORE SUBSTANTIAL OPTION: 92

# Poached Fish Dumplings with Creamy Chilli Sauce

**SERVES 4**

450 g/1 lb white fish fillet, skinned and boned
1 tsp dark soy sauce
1 tbsp cornflour
1 medium egg yolk
salt and freshly ground black pepper
3 tbsp freshly chopped coriander, plus extra, to garnish
1.6 litres/2¾ pints fish stock

**For the creamy chilli sauce:**
2 tsp groundnut oil
2 garlic cloves, peeled and finely chopped
4 spring onions, trimmed and finely sliced

2 tbsp dry sherry
1 tbsp sweet chilli sauce
1 tbsp light soy sauce
1 tbsp lemon juice
6 tbsp crème fraîche

sprigs of fresh coriander, to garnish
fresh carrot sticks, to garnish

Chop the fish into chunks and place in a food processor with the soy sauce, cornflour and egg yolk. Season to taste with salt and pepper. Blend until fairly smooth. Add the coriander and process for a few seconds until well mixed. Transfer to a bowl, cover and chill in the refrigerator for 30 minutes.

With damp hands shape the chilled mixture into walnut-sized balls and place on a baking tray lined with nonstick baking paper. Chill in the refrigerator for a further 30 minutes.

Pour the stock into a wide saucepan, bring to the boil, then reduce the heat until barely simmering. Add the fish balls and poach for 3–4 minutes or until cooked through.

Meanwhile, make the sauce. Heat the oil in a small saucepan, add the garlic and spring onions and cook until golden. Stir in the sherry, chilli and soy sauces and lemon juice, then remove immediately from the heat. Stir in the crème fraîche and season to taste with salt and pepper.

Using a slotted spoon, lift the cooked fish balls from the stock and place on a warmed serving dish. Drizzle over the sauce, garnish with sprigs of fresh coriander and serve immediately.

*Try this:* FOR AN ALTERNATIVE: 54 FOR A MORE SUBSTANTIAL OPTION: 84

# Thai Hot-&-Sour Prawn Soup

**SERVES 6**

700 g/1½ lb large raw prawns
2 tbsp vegetable oil
3–4 stalks lemon grass,
    outer leaves discarded
    and coarsely chopped
2.5 cm/1 inch piece fresh
    root ginger, peeled and
    finely chopped
2–3 garlic cloves, peeled
    and crushed

small bunch fresh coriander,
    leaves stripped and
    reserved, stems
    finely chopped
½ tsp freshly ground
    black pepper
1.8 litres/3¼ pints water
1–2 small red chillies,
    deseeded and
    thinly sliced

1–2 small green chillies,
    deseeded and
    thinly sliced
6 kaffir lime leaves,
    thinly shredded
4 spring onions, trimmed
    and diagonally sliced
1–2 tbsp Thai fish sauce
1–2 tbsp freshly squeezed
    lime juice

Remove the heads from the prawns by twisting away from the body and reserve. Peel the prawns, leaving the tails on and reserve the shells with the heads. Using a sharp knife, remove the black vein from the back of the prawns. Rinse and dry the prawns and reserve. Rinse and dry the heads and shells.

Heat a wok, add the oil and, when hot, add the prawn heads and shells, the lemon grass, ginger, garlic, coriander stems and black pepper and stir-fry for 2–3 minutes, or until the prawn heads and shells turn pink and all the ingredients are coloured.

Carefully add the water to the wok and return to the boil, skimming off any scum which rises to the surface. Simmer over a medium heat for 10 minutes or until slightly reduced. Strain through a fine sieve and return the clear prawn stock to the wok.

Bring the stock back to the boil and add the reserved prawns, chillies, lime leaves and spring onions and simmer for 3 minutes, or until the prawns turn pink. Season with the fish sauce and lime juice. Spoon into heated soup bowls, dividing the prawns evenly and float a few coriander leaves over the surface.

*Try this:* FOR AN ALTERNATIVE: 62  FOR A MORE SUBSTANTIAL OPTION: 344

# Sweetcorn & Crab Soup

**SERVES 4**

450 g/1 lb fresh
corn-on-the-cob
1.3 litres/2¼ pints
chicken stock
2–3 spring onions, trimmed
and finely chopped
1 cm/½ inch piece fresh
root ginger, peeled

and finely chopped
1 tbsp dry sherry or
Chinese rice wine
2–3 tsp soy sauce
1 tsp soft light brown sugar
salt and freshly ground
black pepper
2 tsp cornflour

225 g/8 oz white crabmeat,
fresh or canned
1 medium egg white
1 tsp sesame oil
1–2 tbsp freshly chopped
coriander

Wash the corns cobs and dry. Using a sharp knife and holding the corn cobs at an angle to the cutting board, cut down along the cobs to remove the kernels, then scrape the cobs to remove any excess milky residue. Put the kernels and the milky residue into a large wok.

Add the chicken stock to the wok and place over a high heat. Bring to the boil, stirring and pressing some of the kernels against the side of the wok to squeeze out the starch to help thicken the soup. Simmer for 15 minutes, stirring occasionally.

Add the spring onions, ginger, sherry or Chinese rice wine, soy sauce and brown sugar to the wok and season to taste with salt and pepper. Simmer for a further 5 minutes, stirring occasionally.

Blend the cornflour with 1 tablespoon of cold water to form a smooth paste and whisk into the soup. Return to the boil, then simmer over medium heat until thickened.

Add the crabmeat, stirring until blended. Beat the egg white with the sesame oil and stir into the soup in a slow steady stream, stirring constantly. Stir in the chopped coriander and serve immediately.

*Try this:* FOR AN ALTERNATIVE: 26 FOR A MORE SUBSTANTIAL OPTION: 98

# Hot-&-Sour Soup

**SERVES 4-6**

| | | |
|---|---|---|
| 25 g/1 oz dried Chinese (shiitake) mushrooms | ½ tsp dried crushed chillies | 1–2 tsp sugar |
| 2 tbsp groundnut oil | 1.1 litres/2 pints chicken stock | 3 tbsp cider vinegar |
| 1 carrot, peeled and cut into julienne strips | 75 g/3 oz cooked boneless chicken or pork, shredded | 2 tbsp soy sauce |
| 125 g/4 oz chestnut mushrooms, wiped and thinly sliced | 125 g/4 oz fresh bean curd, thinly sliced, optional | salt and freshly ground black pepper |
| 2 garlic cloves, peeled and finely chopped | 2–3 spring onions, trimmed and finely sliced diagonally | 1 tbsp cornflour |
| | | 1 large egg |
| | | 2 tsp sesame oil |
| | | 2 tbsp freshly chopped coriander |

Place the dried Chinese (shiitake) mushrooms in a small bowl and pour over enough almost boiling water to cover. Leave for 20 minutes to soften, then gently lift out and squeeze out the liquid. (Lifting out the mushrooms leaves any sand and grit behind.) Discard the stems and thinly slice the caps and reserve.

Heat a large wok, add the oil and when hot, add the carrot strips and stir-fry for 2–3 minutes, or until beginning to soften. Add the chestnut mushrooms and stir-fry for 2–3 minutes, or until golden, then stir in the garlic and chillies.

Add the chicken stock to the vegetables and bring to the boil, skimming any foam from the surface. Add the shredded chicken or pork, bean curd, if using, spring onions, sugar, vinegar, soy sauce and mushrooms and simmer for 5 minutes, stirring occasionally. Season to taste.

Blend the cornflour with 1 tablespoon of cold water to form a smooth paste and whisk into the soup. Return to the boil and simmer over a medium heat until thickened. Beat the egg with the sesame oil and slowly add to the soup in a slow, steady stream, stirring constantly. Stir in the chopped coriander and serve the soup immediately.

*Try this:* FOR AN ALTERNATIVE: 58 FOR A MORE SUBSTANTIAL OPTION: 240

# Chinese Leaf & Mushroom Soup

**SERVES 4-6**

450 g/1 lb Chinese leaves
25 g/1 oz dried Chinese (shiitake) mushrooms
1 tbsp vegetable oil
75 g/3 oz smoked streaky bacon, diced
2.5 cm/1 inch piece fresh

root ginger, peeled and finely chopped
175 g/6 oz chestnut mushrooms, thinly sliced
1.1 litres/2 pints chicken stock
4-6 spring onions, trimmed

and cut into short lengths
2 tbsp dry sherry or Chinese rice wine
salt and freshly ground black pepper
sesame oil for drizzling

Trim the stem ends of the Chinese leaves and cut in half lengthways. Remove the triangular core with a knife, then cut into 2.5 cm/1 inch slices and reserve.

Place the dried Chinese mushrooms in a bowl and pour over enough almost boiling water to cover. Leave to stand for 20 minutes to soften, then gently lift out and squeeze out the liquid. Discard the stems and thinly slice the caps and reserve. Strain the liquid through a muslin-lined sieve or a coffee filter paper and reserve.

Heat a wok over a medium-high heat, add the oil and when hot add the bacon. Stir-fry for 3–4 minutes, or until crisp and golden, stirring frequently. Add the ginger and chestnut mushrooms and stir-fry for a further 2–3 minutes.

Add the chicken stock and bring to the boil, skimming any fat and scum that rises to the surface. Add the spring onions, sherry or rice wine, Chinese leaves, sliced Chinese mushrooms and season to taste with salt and pepper. Pour in the reserved soaking liquid and reduce the heat to the lowest possible setting. Simmer gently, covered, until all the vegetables are very tender; this will take about 10 minutes. Add a little water if the liquid has reduced too much. Spoon into soup bowls and drizzle with a little sesame oil. Serve immediately.

*Try this:* FOR AN ALTERNATIVE: 20 FOR A MORE SUBSTANTIAL OPTION: 260

# Laksa Malayan Rice Noodle Soup

**SERVES 4-6**

1.1 kg/2½ lb corn-fed, free-range chicken
1 tsp black peppercorns
1 tbsp vegetable oil
1 large onion, peeled and thinly sliced
2 garlic cloves, peeled and finely chopped
2.5 cm/1 inch piece fresh root ginger, peeled and

thinly sliced
1 tsp ground coriander
2 red chillies, deseeded and diagonally sliced
1–2 tsp hot curry paste
400 ml/14 fl oz coconut milk
450 g/1 lb large raw prawns, peeled and deveined
½ small head of Chinese leaves, thinly shredded

1 tsp sugar
2 spring onions, trimmed and thinly sliced
125 g/4 oz beansprouts
250 g/9 oz rice noodles or rice sticks, soaked as per packet instructions
fresh mint leaves, to garnish

Put the chicken in a large saucepan with the peppercorns and cover with cold water. Bring to the boil, skimming off any scum that rises to the surface. Simmer, partially covered, for about 1 hour. Remove the chicken and cool. Skim any fat from the stock and strain through a muslin-lined sieve and reserve. Remove the meat from the carcass, shred and reserve.

Heat a large wok, add the oil and when hot, add the onions and stir-fry for 2 minutes, or until they begin to colour. Stir in the garlic, ginger, coriander, chillies and curry paste and stir-fry for a further 2 minutes. Carefully pour in the reserved stock (you need at least 1.1 litres/2 pints) and simmer gently, partially covered, for 10 minutes, or until slightly reduced.

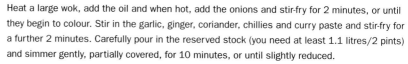

Add the coconut milk, prawns, Chinese leaves, sugar, spring onions and beansprouts and simmer for 3 minutes, stirring occasionally. Add the reserved shredded chicken, and cook for a further 2 minutes.

Drain the noodles and divide between 4–6 soup bowls. Ladle the hot stock and vegetables over the noodles, making sure each serving has some prawns and chicken. Garnish each bowl with fresh mint leaves and serve immediately.

*Try this:* FOR AN ALTERNATIVE: 24 FOR A MORE SUBSTANTIAL OPTION: 280

# Sesame Prawns

**SERVES 6-8**

24 large raw prawns
40 g/1 oz plain flour
4 tbsp sesame seeds
salt and freshly ground
  black pepper
1 large egg

300 ml/½ pint vegetable oil
for deep frying

**For the soy dipping sauce:**
50 ml/2 fl oz soy sauce
1 spring onion, trimmed and

  finely chopped
½ tsp dried crushed chillies
1 tbsp sesame oil
1–2 tsp sugar, or to taste
strips of spring onion,
  to garnish

Remove the heads from the prawns by twisting away from the body and discard. Peel the prawns, leaving the tails on for presentation. Using a sharp knife, remove the black vein from the back of the prawns. Rinse and dry. Slice along the back, but do not cut through the prawn body. Place on the chopping board and press firmly to flatten slightly, to make a butterfly shape.

Put the flour, half the sesame seeds, salt and pepper into a food processor and blend for 30 seconds. Tip into a polythene bag and add the prawns, 4–5 at a time. Twist to seal, then shake to coat with the flour.

Beat the egg in a small bowl with the remaining sesame seeds, salt and pepper.

Heat the oil in a large wok to 190°C/375°F, or until a small cube of bread browns in about 30 seconds. Working in batches of 5 or 6, and holding each prawn by the tail, dip into the beaten egg, then carefully lower into the oil. Cook for 1–2 minutes, or until crisp and golden, turning once or twice. Using a slotted spoon, remove the prawns, drain on absorbent kitchen paper and keep warm.

To make the dipping sauce, stir together the soy sauce, spring onion, chillies, oil and sugar until the sugar dissolves. Arrange the prawns on a plate, garnish with strips of spring onion and serve immediately.

*Try this:* FOR AN ALTERNATIVE: 38 FOR A MORE SUBSTANTIAL OPTION: 122

# Barbecue Pork Steamed Buns

**SERVES 12**

**For the buns:**
175–200 g/6–7 oz plain flour
1 tbsp dried yeast
125 ml/4 fl oz milk
2 tbsp sunflower oil
1 tbsp sugar
½ tsp salt
spring onion tassels,
to garnish
fresh green salad leaves,
to serve

**For the filling:**
2 tbsp vegetable oil
1 small red pepper, deseeded
and finely chopped
2 garlic cloves, peeled
and finely chopped
225 g/8 oz cooked pork,
finely chopped
50 g/2 oz light brown sugar
50 ml/2 fl oz tomato ketchup
1–2 tsp hot chilli powder,
or to taste

Put 75 g/3 oz of the flour in a bowl and stir in the yeast. Heat the milk, oil, sugar and salt in a small saucepan until warm, stirring until the sugar has dissolved. Pour into the bowl and, with an electric mixer, beat on a low speed for 30 seconds, scraping down the sides of the bowl, until blended. Beat at high speed for 3 minutes, then with a wooden spoon, stir in as much of the remaining flour as possible, until a stiff dough forms. Shape into a ball, place in a lightly oiled bowl, cover with clingfilm and leave for 1 hour in a warm place, or until doubled in size.

To make the filling, heat a wok, add the oil and when hot add the red pepper and garlic. Stir-fry for 4–5 minutes. Add the remaining ingredients and bring to the boil, stir-frying for 2–3 minutes until thick and syrupy. Cool and reserve. Punch down the dough and turn onto a lightly floured surface. Divide into 12 pieces and shape into balls, then cover and leave to rest for 5 minutes. Roll each ball to a 7.5 cm/3 inch circle. Place a heaped tablespoon of filling in the centre of each. Dampen the edges, then bring them up and around the filling, pinching together to seal. Place seam-side down on a small square of non-stick baking parchment. Continue with the remaining dough and filling. Leave to rise for 10 minutes. Bring a large wok half-filled with water to the boil, place the buns in a lightly oiled Chinese steamer, without touching each other. Cover and steam for 20–25 minutes, then remove and cool slightly. Garnish with spring onion tassels and serve with salad leaves.

*Try this:* FOR AN ALTERNATIVE: 44 FOR A MORE SUBSTANTIAL OPTION: 150

# Chicken–filled Spring Rolls

**MAKES 12-14 ROLLS**

**For the filling:**
1 tbsp vegetable oil
2 slices streaky bacon, diced
225 g/8 oz skinless chicken
　　breast fillets, thinly sliced
1 small red pepper,
　　deseeded and
　　finely chopped
4 spring onions, trimmed
　　and finely chopped

2.5 cm/1 inch piece fresh
　　root ginger, peeled and
　　finely chopped
75 g/3 oz mangetout peas,
　　thinly sliced
75 g/3 oz beansprouts
1 tbsp soy sauce
2 tsp Chinese rice wine or
　　dry sherry
2 tsp hoisin or plum sauce

**For the wrappers:**
3 tbsp plain flour
12–14 spring roll wrappers
300 ml/½ pint vegetable oil
　　for deep frying
shredded spring onions,
　　to garnish
dipping sauce, to serve

Heat a large wok, add the oil and when hot add the diced bacon and stir-fry for 2–3 minutes, or until golden. Add the chicken and pepper and stir-fry for a further 2–3 minutes. Add the remaining filling ingredients and stir-fry 3–4 minutes until all the vegetables are tender. Turn into a colander and leave to drain as the mixture cools completely.

Blend the flour with about 1½ tablespoons of water to form a paste. Soften each wrapper in a plate of warm water for 1–2 seconds, then place on a chopping board. Put 2–3 tablespoons of filling on the near edge. Fold the edge over the filling to cover. Fold in each side and roll up. Seal the edge with a little flour paste and press to seal securely. Transfer to a baking sheet, seam-side down.

Heat the oil in a large wok to 190°C/375°F, or until a small cube of bread browns in about 30 seconds. Working in batches of 3–4, fry the spring rolls until they are crisp and golden, turning once (about 2 minutes). Remove and drain on absorbent kitchen paper. Arrange the spring rolls on a serving plate, garnish with spring onion tassels and serve hot with dipping sauce.

*Try this:* FOR AN ALTERNATIVE: 52 FOR A MORE SUBSTANTIAL OPTION: 160

# Prawn Salad
# with Toasted Rice

**SERVES 4**

**For the dressing:**
50 ml/2 fl oz rice vinegar
1 red chilli, deseeded and
    thinly sliced
7.5 cm/3 inch piece lemon
    grass stalk, bruised
juice of 1 lime
2 tbsp Thai fish sauce
1 tsp sugar, or to taste

**For the salad:**
350 g/12 oz large raw
    prawns, peeled with tails
    attached, heads removed
cayenne pepper
1 tbsp long-grain white rice
salt and freshly ground
    black pepper
2 tbsp sunflower oil

1 large head Chinese leaves
    or cos lettuce, shredded
½ small cucumber,
    peeled, deseeded
    and thinly sliced
1 small bunch chives, cut
    into 2.5 cm/1 inch pieces
small bunch of mint leaves

Place all the ingredients for the dressing in a small bowl and leave to stand to let the flavours blend together.

Using a sharp knife, split each prawn lengthways in half, leaving the tail attached to one half. Remove any black vein and pat the prawns dry with absorbent kitchen paper. Sprinkle the prawns with a little salt and cayenne pepper and then reserve.

Heat a wok over a high heat. Add the rice and stir-fry until browned and fragrant. Turn into a mortar and cool. Crush gently with a pestle until coarse crumbs form. Wipe the wok clean.

Reheat the wok, add the oil and when hot, add the prawns and stir-fry for 2 minutes, or until pink. Transfer to a plate and season to taste with salt and pepper.

Place the Chinese leaves or lettuce into a salad bowl with the cucumber, chives and mint leaves and toss lightly together. Remove the lemon grass stalk and some of the chilli from the dressing and pour all but 2 tablespoons over the salad and toss until lightly coated. Add the prawns and drizzle with the remaining dressing, then sprinkle with the toasted rice and serve.

*Try this:* FOR AN ALTERNATIVE: 48 FOR A MORE SUBSTANTIAL OPTION: 286

# Sticky Braised Spare Ribs

**SERVES 4**

900 g/2 lb meaty pork spare
  ribs, cut crossways into
  7.5 cm/3 inch pieces
125 ml/4 fl oz apricot nectar
  or orange juice
50 ml/2 fl oz dry white wine
3 tbsp black bean sauce

3 tbsp tomato ketchup
2 tbsp clear honey
3–4 spring onions, trimmed
  and chopped
2 garlic cloves, peeled
  and crushed
grated zest of 1 small orange

salt and freshly ground
  black pepper
spring onion tassels,
  to garnish
lemon wedges, to garnish

Put the spare ribs in the wok and add enough cold water to cover. Bring to the boil over a medium-high heat, skimming any scum that rises to the surface. Cover and simmer for 30 minutes, then drain and rinse the ribs.

Rinse and dry the wok and return the ribs to it. In a bowl, blend the apricot nectar or orange juice with the white wine, black bean sauce, tomato ketchup and the honey until smooth.

Stir in the spring onions, garlic cloves and grated orange zest. Stir well until mixed thoroughly.

Pour the mixture over the spare ribs in the wok and stir gently until the ribs are lightly coated. Place over a moderate heat and bring to the boil.

Cover then simmer, stirring occasionally, for 1 hour, or until the ribs are tender and the sauce is thickened and sticky. (If the sauce reduces too quickly or begins to stick, add water 1 tablespoon at a time until the ribs are tender.) Adjust the seasoning to taste, then transfer the ribs to a serving plate and garnish with spring onion tassels and lemon wedges. Serve immediately.

*Try this:* FOR AN ALTERNATIVE: 32  FOR A MORE SUBSTANTIAL OPTION: 166

# Soy-glazed Chicken Thighs

**SERVES 6-8**

900 g/2 lb chicken thighs
2 tbsp vegetable oil
3–4 garlic cloves, peeled
    and crushed
4 cm/1½ inch piece fresh
    root ginger, peeled and

finely chopped or grated
125 ml/4 fl oz soy sauce
2–3 tbsp Chinese rice wine
    or dry sherry
2 tbsp clear honey
1 tbsp soft brown sugar

2–3 dashes hot chilli sauce,
    or to taste
freshly chopped parsley,
    to garnish

Heat a large wok and when hot add the oil and heat. Stir-fry the chicken thighs for 5 minutes or until golden. Remove and drain on absorbent kitchen paper. You may need to do this in 2–3 batches.

Pour off the oil and fat and, using absorbent kitchen paper, carefully wipe out the wok. Add the garlic, with the root ginger, soy sauce, Chinese rice wine or sherry and honey to the wok and stir well. Sprinkle in the soft brown sugar with the hot chilli sauce to taste, then place over the heat and bring to the boil.

Reduce the heat to a gentle simmer, then carefully add the chicken thighs. Cover the wok and simmer gently over a very low heat for 30 minutes, or until they are tender and the sauce is reduced and thickened and glazes the chicken thighs.

Stir or spoon the sauce occasionally over the chicken thighs and add a little water if the sauce is starting to become too thick. Arrange in a shallow serving dish, garnish with freshly chopped parsley and serve immediately.

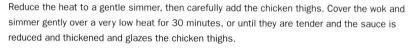

*Try this:* FOR AN ALTERNATIVE: 50 FOR A MORE SUBSTANTIAL OPTION: 208

# Shredded Duck in Lettuce Leaves

**SERVES 4-6**

15 g/1⁄2 oz dried Chinese (shiitake) mushrooms
2 tbsp vegetable oil
400 g/14 oz boneless, skinless duck breast, cut crossways into thin strips
1 red chilli, deseeded and diagonally thinly sliced

4–6 spring onions, trimmed and diagonally sliced
2 garlic cloves, peeled and crushed
75 g/3 oz beansprouts
3 tbsp soy sauce
1 tbsp Chinese rice wine or dry sherry

1–2 tsp clear honey or brown sugar
4–6 tbsp hoisin sauce
large, crisp lettuce leaves such as iceberg or cos
handful of fresh mint leaves
dipping sauce (see Sesame Prawns, page 68)

Cover the dried Chinese mushrooms with almost boiling water, leave for 20 minutes, then drain and slice thinly. Heat a large wok, add the oil and when hot stir-fry the duck for 3–4 minutes, or until sealed. Remove with a slotted spoon and reserve.

Add the chilli, spring onions, garlic and Chinese mushrooms to the wok and stir-fry for 2–3 minutes, or until softened. Add the beansprouts, the soy sauce, Chinese rice wine or dry sherry and honey or brown sugar to the wok, and continue to stir-fry for 1 minute, or until blended.

Stir in the reserved duck and stir-fry for 2 minutes, or until well mixed together and heated right through. Transfer to a heated serving dish.

Arrange the hoisin sauce in a small bowl on a tray or plate with a pile of lettuce leaves and the mint leaves. Let each guest spoon a little hoisin sauce onto a lettuce leaf, then top with a large spoonful of the stir-fried duck and vegetables and roll up the leaf to enclose the filling. Serve with the dipping sauce.

*Try this:* FOR AN ALTERNATIVE: 48  FOR A MORE SUBSTANTIAL OPTION: 200

# Fish & Shellfish

# Steamed Monkfish with Chilli & Ginger

**SERVES 4**

700 g/1½ lb skinless
   monkfish tail
1–2 red chillies
4 cm/1½ inch piece fresh
   root ginger
1 tsp sesame oil

4 spring onions, trimmed
   and thinly sliced
   diagonally
2 tbsp soy sauce
2 tbsp Chinese rice wine
   or dry sherry

freshly steamed rice,
   to serve
sprigs of fresh coriander,
   to garnish
lime wedges

Place the monkfish on a chopping board. Using a sharp knife, cut down each side of the central bone and remove. Cut the fish into 2.5cm/1 inch pieces and reserve.

Make a slit down the side of each chilli, remove and discard the seeds and the membrane, then slice thinly. Peel the ginger and either chop finely or grate.

Brush a large heatproof plate with the sesame oil and arrange the monkfish pieces in one layer on the plate. Sprinkle over the spring onions and pour over the soy sauce and Chinese rice wine or sherry. Place a wire rack or inverted ramekin in a large wok. Pour in enough water to come about 2.5 cm/1 inch up the side of the wok and bring to the boil over a high heat.

Fold a long piece of tinfoil lengthways to about 5–7.5 cm/2–3 inches wide and lay it over the rack or ramekin. It must extend beyond the plate edge when it is placed in the wok. Place the plate with the monkfish on the rack or ramekin and cover tightly. Steam over a medium-low heat for 5 minutes, or until the fish is tender and opaque. Using the tinfoil as a hammock, lift out the plate. Garnish with sprigs of coriander and lime wedges and serve immediately with steamed rice.

*Try this:* FOR AN ALTERNATIVE: 114  FOR A LIGHT BITE: 56

# Red Prawn Curry with Jasmine–scented rice

**SERVES 4**

½ tbsp coriander seeds
1 tsp cumin seeds
1 tsp black peppercorns
½ tsp salt
1–2 dried red chillies
2 shallots, peeled and chopped
3–4 garlic cloves
2.5 cm/1 inch piece fresh galangal or root ginger, peeled and chopped
1 kaffir lime leaf or 1 tsp

kaffir lime rind
½ tsp red chilli powder
½ tbsp shrimp paste
1–1½ lemon grass stalks, outer leaves removed and thinly sliced
750 ml/1¼ pints coconut milk
1 red chilli deseeded and thinly sliced
2 tbsp Thai fish sauce
2 tsp soft brown sugar
1 red pepper, deseeded and

thinly sliced
550 g/1¼ lb large peeled tiger prawns
2 fresh lime leaves, shredded (optional)
2 tbsp fresh mint leaves, shredded
2 tbsp Thai or Italian basil leaves, shredded
freshly cooked Thai fragrant rice, to serve

Using a pestle and mortar or a spice grinder, grind the coriander and cumin seeds, peppercorns and salt to a fine powder. Add the dried chillies one at a time and grind to a fine powder.

Place the shallots, garlic, galangal or ginger, kaffir lime leaf or rind, chilli powder and shrimp paste in a food processor. Add the ground spices and process until a thick paste forms. Scrape down the bowl once or twice, adding a few drops of water if the mixture is too thick and not forming a paste. Stir in the lemon grass.

Transfer the paste to a large wok and cook over a medium heat for 2–3 minutes or until fragrant. Stir in the coconut milk, bring to the boil, then lower the heat and simmer for about 10 minutes. Add the chilli, fish sauce, sugar and red pepper and simmer for 15 minutes.

Stir in the prawns and cook for 5 minutes, or until the prawns are pink and tender. Stir in the shredded herbs, heat for a further minute and serve immediately with the cooked rice.

*Try this:* FOR AN ALTERNATIVE: 126  FOR A LIGHT BITE: 26

# Thai Prawn & Rice Noodle Salad

**SERVES 4**

75 g/3 oz rice vermicelli
175 g/6 oz mangetout, cut in half crossways
½ cucumber, peeled, deseeded and diced
2–3 spring onions, trimmed and thinly sliced diagonally
16–20 large cooked tiger prawns, peeled with tails left on
2 tbsp chopped unsalted peanuts or cashews

**For the dressing:**
4 tbsp freshly squeezed lime juice
3 tbsp Thai fish sauce
1 tbsp sugar
2.5 cm/1 inch piece fresh root ginger, peeled and finely chopped
1 red chilli, deseeded and thinly sliced
3–4 tbsp freshly chopped coriander or mint

lime wedges, to garnish
sprigs of fresh mint, to garnish

Place the vermicelli in a bowl and pour over hot water to cover. Leave to stand for 5 minutes or until softened. Drain, rinse, then drain again and reserve.

Meanwhile, mix all the dressing ingredients in a large bowl until well blended and the sugar has dissolved. Reserve.

Bring a medium saucepan of water to the boil. Add the mangetout, return to the boil and cook for 30–50 seconds. Drain, refresh under cold running water, drain again and reserve.

Stir the cucumber, spring onions and all but 4 of the prawns into the dressing until coated lightly. Add the mangetout and noodles and toss until all the ingredients are mixed evenly.

Spoon the noodle salad on to warmed individual plates. Sprinkle with peanuts or cashews and garnish each dish with a reserved prawn, a lime wedge and a sprig of mint.

*Try this:* FOR AN ALTERNATIVE: 282  FOR A LIGHT BITE: 74

# Thai Curried Seafood

**SERVES 6-8**

2 tbsp vegetable oil
450 g/1 lb scallops, with coral attached if preferred, halved if large
1 onion, peeled and finely chopped
4 garlic cloves, peeled and finely chopped
5 cm/2 inch piece fresh root ginger, peeled and finely chopped
1–2 red chillies, deseeded and thinly sliced
1–2 tbsp curry paste (hot or medium, to taste)
1 tsp ground coriander
1 tsp ground cumin
1 lemon grass stalk, bruised
225 g can chopped tomatoes
125 ml/4 fl oz chicken stock or water
450 ml/ ¾ pint coconut milk
12 live mussels, scrubbed and beards removed
450 g/1 lb cooked peeled prawns
225 g/8 oz frozen or canned crabmeat, drained
2 tbsp freshly chopped coriander
freshly shredded coconut, to garnish (optional)
freshly cooked rice or rice noodles, to serve

Heat a wok or large frying pan, add 1 tablespoon of the oil and when hot, add the scallops and stir-fry for 2 minutes or until opaque and firm. Transfer to a plate with any juices.

Heat the remaining oil. Add the onion, garlic, ginger and chillies and stir-fry for 1 minute or until they begin to soften.

Add the curry paste, coriander, cumin and lemon grass and stir-fry for 2 minutes. Add the tomatoes and stock, bring to the boil then simmer for 5 minutes or until reduced, stirring constantly. Stir in the coconut milk and simmer for 2 minutes.

Stir in the mussels, cover and simmer for 2 minutes or until they begin to open. Stir in the prawns, crabmeat and reserved scallops with any juices and cook for 2 minutes or until heated through. Discard the lemon grass and any unopened mussels. Stir in the chopped coriander. Tip into a large warmed serving dish and garnish with the coconut, if using. Serve immediately with rice or noodles.

*Try this:* FOR AN ALTERNATIVE: 86  FOR A LIGHT BITE: 48

# Fried Fish with Thai Chilli Dipping Sauce

**SERVES 4**

1 large egg white
½ tsp curry powder or turmeric
3–4 tbsp cornflour
salt and freshly ground black pepper
4 plaice or sole fillets, about 225 g/8 oz each
300 ml/ ½ pint vegetable oil

**For the dipping sauce:**
2 red chillies, deseeded and thinly sliced
2 shallots, peeled and finely chopped
1 tbsp freshly squeezed lime juice
3 tbsp Thai fish sauce

1 tbsp freshly chopped coriander or Thai basil

freshly cooked rice, to serve
mixed salad leaves, to serve

To make the dipping sauce, combine all the ingredients in a bowl. Leave for at least 15 minutes.

Beat the egg white until frothy and whisk into a shallow dish.

Stir the curry powder or turmeric into the cornflour in a bowl and season to taste with salt and pepper. Dip each fish fillet in the beaten egg white, dust lightly on both sides with the cornflour mixture and place on a wire rack.

Heat a wok or large frying pan, add the oil and heat to 180°C/350°F. Add 1 or 2 fillets and fry for 5 minutes, or until crisp and golden, turning once during cooking. Using a slotted spatula, carefully remove the cooked fish and drain on absorbent kitchen paper. Keep warm while frying the remaining fillets.

Arrange the fillets on warmed individual plates and serve immediately with the dipping sauce, rice and salad.

*Try this:* FOR AN ALTERNATIVE: 110  FOR A LIGHT BITE: 54

# Scallops & Prawns Braised in Lemon Grass

**SERVES 4-6**

450 g/1 lb large raw prawns, peeled with tails left on
350 g/12 oz scallops, with coral attached
2 red chillies, deseeded and coarsely chopped
2 garlic cloves, peeled and coarsely chopped
4 shallots, peeled
1 tbsp shrimp paste
2 tbsp freshly chopped coriander
400 ml/14 fl oz coconut milk
2–3 lemon grass stalks, outer leaves discarded and bruised
2 tbsp Thai fish sauce
1 tbsp sugar
freshly steamed basmati rice, to serve

Rinse the prawns and scallops and pat dry with absorbent kitchen paper. Using a sharp knife, remove the black vein along the back of the prawns. Reserve.

Place the chillies, garlic, shallots, shrimp paste and 1 tablespoon of the chopped coriander in a food processor. Add 1 tablespoon of the coconut milk and 2 tablespoons of water and blend to form a thick paste. Reserve the chilli paste.

Pour the remaining coconut milk with 3 tablespoons of water into a large wok or frying pan, add the lemon grass and bring to the boil. Simmer over a medium heat for 10 minutes or until reduced slightly.

Stir the chilli paste, fish sauce and sugar into the coconut milk and continue to simmer for 2 minutes, stirring occasionally.

Add the prepared prawns and scallops and simmer gently, for 3 minutes, stirring occasionally, or until cooked and the prawns are pink and the scallops are opaque.

Remove the lemon grass and stir in the remaining chopped coriander. Serve immediately spooned over freshly steamed basmati rice.

*Try this:* FOR AN ALTERNATIVE: 132   FOR A LIGHT BITE: 46

# Fragrant Thai Swordfish with Peppers

**SERVES 4-6**

550 g/1¼ lb swordfish, cut into 5 cm/2 inch strips
2 tbsp vegetable oil
2 lemon grass stalks, peeled, bruised and cut into 2.5 cm/1 inch pieces
2.5 cm/1 inch piece fresh root ginger, peeled and thinly sliced
4–5 shallots, peeled and thinly sliced
2–3 garlic cloves, peeled and thinly sliced
1 small red pepper, deseeded and thinly sliced
1 small yellow pepper, deseeded and thinly sliced
2 tbsp soy sauce
2 tbsp Chinese rice wine or dry sherry
1–2 tsp sugar
1 tsp sesame oil
1 tbsp Thai or Italian basil, shredded
salt and freshly ground black pepper
1 tbsp toasted sesame seeds

**For the marinade:**
1 tbsp soy sauce
1 tbsp Chinese rice wine or dry sherry
1 tbsp sesame oil
1 tbsp cornflour

Blend all the marinade ingredients together in a shallow, nonmetallic baking dish. Add the swordfish and spoon the marinade over the fish. Cover and leave to marinate in the refrigerator for at least 30 minutes.

Using a slotted spatula or spoon, remove the fish from the marinade and drain on absorbent kitchen paper. Heat a wok or large frying pan, add the oil and when hot, add the fish and stir-fry for 2 minutes, or until it begins to brown. Remove and drain on absorbent kitchen paper.

Add the lemon grass, ginger, shallots and garlic to the wok and stir-fry for 30 seconds. Add the peppers, soy sauce, Chinese rice wine or sherry and sugar and stir-fry for 3–4 minutes.

Return the swordfish to the wok and stir-fry gently for 1–2 minutes, or until heated through and coated with the sauce. If necessary, moisten the sauce with a little of the marinade or some water. Stir in the sesame oil and the basil and season to taste with salt and pepper. Tip into a warmed serving bowl, sprinkle with sesame seeds and serve immediately.

*Try this:* FOR AN ALTERNATIVE: 176   FOR A LIGHT BITE: 36

# Thai Coconut Crab Curry

**SERVES 4-6**

1 onion
4 garlic cloves
5 cm/2 inch piece fresh
    root ginger
2 tbsp vegetable oil
2–3 tsp hot curry paste

400 g/14 oz coconut milk
2 large dressed crabs, white
    and dark meat separated
2 lemon grass stalks, peeled
    and bruised
6 spring onions, trimmed

and chopped
2 tbsp freshly shredded Thai
    basil or mint, plus extra,
    to garnish
freshly boiled rice, to serve

Peel the onion and chop finely. Peel the garlic cloves, then either crush or finely chop. Peel the ginger and either grate coarsely or cut into very thin shreds. Reserve.

Heat a wok or large frying pan, add the oil and when hot, add the onion, garlic and ginger and stir-fry for 2 minutes, or until the onion is beginning to soften. Stir in the curry paste and stir-fry for 1 minute.

Stir the coconut milk into the vegetable mixture with the dark crabmeat. Add the lemon grass, then bring the mixture slowly to the boil, stirring frequently.

Add the spring onions and simmer gently for 15 minutes or until the sauce has thickened. Remove and discard the lemon grass stalks.

Add the white crabmeat and the shredded basil or mint and stir very gently for 1–2 minutes or until heated through and piping hot. Try to prevent the crabmeat from breaking up.

Spoon the curry over boiled rice on warmed individual plates, sprinkle with basil or mint leaves and serve immediately.

*Try this:* FOR AN ALTERNATIVE: 124  FOR A LIGHT BITE: 36

# Thai Marinated Prawns

**SERVES 4**

700 g/1½ lb large raw prawns, peeled with tails left on
2 large eggs
salt
50 g/2 oz cornflour
vegetable oil for deep-frying
lime wedges, to garnish

**For the marinade:**
2 lemon grass stalks, outer leaves discarded and bruised
2 garlic cloves, peeled and finely chopped
2 shallots, peeled and

finely chopped
1 red chilli, deseeded and chopped
grated zest and juice of 1 small lime
400 ml/14 fl oz coconut milk

Mix all the marinade ingredients together in a bowl, pressing on the solid ingredients to release their flavours. Season to taste with salt and reserve.

Using a sharp knife, remove the black vein along the back of the prawns and pat dry with absorbent kitchen paper. Add the prawns to the marinade and stir gently until coated evenly. Leave in the marinade for at least 1 hour, stirring occasionally.

Beat the eggs in a deep bowl with a little salt. Place the cornflour in a shallow bowl. Using a slotted spoon or spatula, transfer the prawns from the marinade to the cornflour. Stir gently until the prawns are coated on all sides and shake off any excess.

Holding each prawn by its tail, dip it into the beaten egg, then into the cornflour again, shaking off any excess.

Pour enough oil into a large wok to come 5 cm/2 inches up the sides and place over a high heat. Working in batches of 5 or 6, deep-fry the prawns for 2 minutes, or until pink and crisp, turning once. Using a slotted spoon, remove and drain on absorbent kitchen paper. Keep warm. Arrange on a warmed serving plate and garnish with lime wedges. Serve immediately.

*Try this:* FOR AN ALTERNATIVE: 134   FOR A LIGHT BITE: 68

# Warm Lobster Salad with Hot Thai Dressing

**SERVES 4**

1 orange
50 g/2 oz granulated sugar
2 Cos lettuce hearts, shredded
1 small avocado, peeled and
    thinly sliced
½ cucumber, peeled, deseeded
    and thinly sliced
1 ripe mango, peeled,
    stoned and thinly sliced
1 tbsp butter or vegetable oil
1 large lobster, meat
    removed and cut into

bite-sized pieces
2 tbsp Thai or Italian basil
    leaves
4 large cooked prawns,
    peeled with tails left on,
    to garnish

**For the dressing:**
1 tbsp vegetable oil
4–6 spring onions, trimmed
    and sliced diagonally into
    5 cm/2 inch pieces

2.5 cm/1 inch piece fresh
    root ginger, peeled and
    grated
1 garlic clove, peeled
    and crushed
grated zest of 1 lime
juice of 2–3 small limes
2 tbsp Thai fish sauce
1 tbsp brown sugar
1–2 tsp sweet chilli sauce,
    or to taste
1 tbsp sesame oil

With a sharp knife, cut the orange rind into thin julienne strips, then cook in boiling water for 2 minutes. Drain the orange strips, then plunge into cold running water, drain and return to the saucepan with the sugar and 1 cm/½ inch water. Simmer until soft, then add 1 tablespoon of cold water to stop cooking. Remove from the heat and reserve. Arrange the lettuce on 4 large plates and arrange the avocado, cucumber and mango slices over the lettuce.

Heat a wok or large frying pan, add the butter or oil and when hot, but not sizzling, add the lobster and stir-fry for 1–2 minutes or until heated through. Remove and drain on absorbent kitchen paper.

To make the dressing, heat the vegetable oil in a wok, then add the spring onions, ginger and garlic and stir-fry for 1 minute. Add the lime zest, lime juice, fish sauce, sugar and chilli sauce. Stir until the sugar dissolves. Remove from the heat, add the sesame oil with the orange rind and liquor. Arrange the lobster meat over the salad and drizzle with dressing. Sprinkle with basil leaves, garnish with prawns and serve immediately.

*Try this:* FOR AN ALTERNATIVE: 352   FOR A LIGHT BITE: 46

# Deep–fried Crab Wontons

**MAKES 24-30**

2 tbsp sesame oil
6–8 water chestnuts, rinsed, drained and chopped
2 spring onions, peeled and finely chopped
1 cm/½ inch piece fresh root ginger, peeled and grated
185 g can white crabmeat,
drained
50 ml/2 fl oz soy sauce
2 tbsp rice wine vinegar
½ tsp dried crushed chillies
2 tsp sugar
½ tsp hot pepper sauce, or to taste
1 tbsp freshly chopped
coriander or dill
1 large egg yolk
1 packet wonton skins
vegetable oil for deep-frying
lime wedges, to garnish
dipping sauce, to serve
(see page 54)

Heat a wok or large frying pan, add 1 tablespoon of the sesame oil and when hot, add the water chestnuts, spring onions and ginger and stir-fry for 1 minute. Remove from the heat and leave to cool slightly. In a bowl, mix the crabmeat with the soy sauce, rice wine vinegar, crushed chillies, sugar, hot pepper sauce, chopped coriander or dill and the egg yolk. Stir in the cooled stir-fried mixture until well blended.

Lay the wonton skins on a work surface and place 1 teaspoonful of the crab mixture on the centre of each. Brush the edges of each wonton skin with a little water and fold up 1 corner to the opposite corner to form a triangle. Press to seal. Bring the 2 corners of the triangle together to meet in the centre, brush 1 with a little water and overlap them, pressing to seal and form a 'tortellini' shape. Place on a baking sheet and continue with the remaining triangles.

Pour enough oil into a large wok to come 5 cm/2 inches up the sides and place over a high heat. Working in batches of 5 or 6, fry the wontons for 3 minutes, or until crisp and golden, turning once or twice. Carefully remove the wontons with a slotted spoon, drain on absorbent kitchen paper and keep warm. Place on individual warmed serving plates, garnish each dish with a lime wedge and serve immediately with the dipping sauce.

*Try this:* FOR AN ALTERNATIVE: 252  FOR A LIGHT BITE: 30

# Szechuan Chilli Prawns

**SERVES 4**

450 g/1 lb raw tiger prawns
2 tbsp groundnut oil
1 onion, peeled and sliced
1 red pepper, deseeded and
   cut into strips
1 small red chilli, deseeded
   and thinly sliced
2 garlic cloves, peeled and

   finely chopped
2–3 spring onions, trimmed
   and diagonally sliced
freshly cooked rice or
   noodles, to serve
sprigs of fresh coriander or
   chilli flowers, to garnish

**For the chilli sauce:**
1 tbsp cornflour
4 tbsp cold fish stock
   or water
2 tbsp soy sauce
2 tbsp sweet or hot chilli
   sauce, or to taste
2 tsp soft light brown sugar

Peel the prawns, leaving the tails attached if you like. Using a sharp knife, remove the black vein along the back of the prawns. Rinse and pat dry with absorbent kitchen paper.

Heat a wok or large frying pan, add the oil and when hot, add the onion, pepper and chilli and stir-fry for 4–5 minutes, or until the vegetables are tender but retain a bite. Stir in the garlic and cook for 30 seconds. Using a slotted spoon, transfer to a plate and reserve.

Add the prawns to the wok and stir-fry for 1–2 minutes, or until they turn pink and opaque.

Blend all the chilli sauce ingredients together in a bowl or jug, then stir into the prawns. Add the reserved vegetables and bring to the boil, stirring constantly. Cook for 1–2 minutes, or until the sauce is thickened and the prawns and vegetables are well coated.

Stir in the spring onions, tip on to a warmed platter and garnish with chilli flowers or coriander sprigs. Serve immediately with freshly cooked rice or noodles.

*Try this:* FOR AN ALTERNATIVE: 122  FOR A LIGHT BITE: 58

# Chinese Steamed Sea Bass with Black Beans

**SERVES 4**

1.1 kg/2½ lb sea bass, cleaned with head and tail left on
1–2 tbsp rice wine or dry sherry
1½ tbsp groundnut oil
2–3 tbsp fermented black beans, rinsed and drained

1 garlic clove, peeled and finely chopped
1 cm/½ inch piece fresh root ginger, peeled and finely chopped
4 spring onions, trimmed and thinly sliced diagonally

2–3 tbsp soy sauce
125 ml/4 fl oz fish or chicken stock
1–2 tbsp sweet Chinese chilli sauce, or to taste
2 tsp sesame oil
sprigs of fresh coriander, to garnish

Using a sharp knife, cut 3–4 deep diagonal slashes along both sides of the fish. Sprinkle the Chinese rice wine or sherry inside and over the fish and gently rub into the skin on both sides.

Lightly brush a heatproof plate large enough to fit into a large wok or frying pan with a little of the groundnut oil. Place the fish on the plate, curving the fish along the inside edge of the dish, then leave for 20 minutes.

Place a wire rack or inverted ramekin in the wok and pour in enough water to come about 2.5 cm/1 inch up the side. Bring to the boil over a high heat. Carefully place the plate with the fish on the rack or ramekin, cover and steam for 12–15 minutes, or until the fish is tender and the flesh is opaque when pierced with a knife near the bone.

Remove the plate with the fish from the wok and keep warm. Remove the rack or ramekin from the wok and pour off the water. Return the wok to the heat, add the remaining groundnut oil and swirl to coat the bottom and side. Add the black beans, garlic and ginger and stir-fry for 1 minute. Add the spring onions, soy sauce, fish or chicken stock and boil for 1 minute. Stir in the chilli sauce and sesame oil, then pour the sauce over the cooked fish. Garnish with coriander sprigs and serve immediately.

*Try this:* FOR AN ALTERNATIVE: 120  FOR A LIGHT BITE: 40

# Sweet-&-Sour Fish

**SERVES 4**

125 g/4 oz carrot, peeled and cut into julienne strips
125 g/4 oz red or green pepper
125 g/4 oz mangetout, cut in half diagonally
125 g/4 oz frozen peas, thawed
2–3 spring onions, trimmed and sliced diagonally into 5 cm/2 inch pieces
450 g/1 lb small thin skinless plaice fillets
1½–2 tbsp cornflour
vegetable oil for frying
sprigs of fresh coriander, to garnish

**For the sweet-&-sour sauce:**
2 tsp cornflour
300 ml/½ pint fish or chicken stock
4 cm/1½ inch piece fresh root ginger, peeled and finely sliced
2 tbsp soy sauce
2 tbsp rice wine vinegar or dry sherry
2 tbsp tomato ketchup or tomato concentrate
2 tbsp Chinese rice vinegar or cider vinegar
1½ tbsp soft light brown sugar

Make the sauce. Place the cornflour in a saucepan and gradually whisk in the stock. Stir in the remaining sauce ingredients and bring to the boil, stirring, until the sauce thickens. Simmer for 2 minutes, then remove from the heat and reserve.

Bring a saucepan of water to the boil. Add the carrot, return to the boil and cook for 3 minutes. Add the pepper and cook for 1 minute. Add the mange-tout and peas and cook for 30 seconds. Drain, rinse under cold running water and drain again, then add to the sweet and sour sauce with the spring onions.

Using a sharp knife, make crisscross slashes across the top of each fish fillet then lightly coat on both sides with the cornflour. Pour enough oil into a large wok to come 5 cm/2 inches up the side. Heat to 190˚C/375˚F, or until a cube of bread browns in 30 seconds. Fry the fish fillets, 2 at a time, for 3–5 minutes, or until crisp and golden, turning once. Using a fish slice, remove and drain on absorbent kitchen paper. Keep warm. Bring the sweet and sour sauce to the boil, stirring constantly. Arrange the fish fillets on a warmed platter and pour over the hot sauce. Garnish with sprigs of coriander and serve immediately.

*Try this:* FOR AN ALTERNATIVE: 326 FOR A LIGHT BITE: 40

# Fish Balls in Hot Yellow Bean Sauce

**SERVES 4**

450 g/1 lb skinless white fish
fillets, such as cod or
haddock, cut into pieces
½ tsp salt
1 tbsp cornflour
2 spring onions, trimmed
and chopped
1 tbsp freshly chopped
coriander

1 tsp soy sauce
1 medium egg white
freshly ground black pepper
sprig of tarragon, to garnish
freshly cooked rice, to serve

**For the yellow bean sauce:**
75 ml/3 fl oz fish or
chicken stock

1–2 tsp yellow bean sauce
2 tbsp soy sauce
1–2 tbsp Chinese rice wine
or dry sherry
1 tsp chilli bean sauce, or
to taste
1 tsp sesame oil
1 tsp sugar (optional)

Put the fish pieces, salt, cornflour, spring onions, coriander, soy sauce and egg white into a food processor, season to taste with pepper, then blend until a smooth paste forms, scraping down the sides of the bowl occasionally.

With dampened hands, shape the mixture into 2.5 cm/1 inch balls. Transfer to a baking tray and chill in the refrigerator for at least 30 minutes.

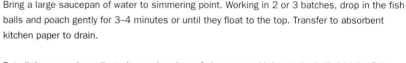

Bring a large saucepan of water to simmering point. Working in 2 or 3 batches, drop in the fish balls and poach gently for 3–4 minutes or until they float to the top. Transfer to absorbent kitchen paper to drain.

Put all the sauce ingredients in a wok or large frying pan and bring to the boil. Add the fish balls to the sauce and stir-fry gently for 2–3 minutes until piping hot. Transfer to a warmed serving dish, garnish with sprigs of tarragon and serve immediately with freshly cooked rice.

 *Try this:* FOR AN ALTERNATIVE: 120 FOR A LIGHT BITE: 56

# Steamed Whole Trout with Ginger & Spring Onion

**SERVES 4**

2 x 450–700 g/1–1½ lb whole trout, gutted with heads removed
coarse sea salt
2 tbsp groundnut oil
½ tbsp soy sauce
1 tbsp sesame oil

2 garlic cloves, peeled and thinly sliced
2.5 cm/1 inch piece fresh root ginger, peeled and thinly slivered
2 spring onions, trimmed and thinly sliced

   diagonally
chive leaves, to garnish
lemon slices, to garnish
freshly cooked rice, to serve
Oriental salad, to serve

Wipe the fish inside and out with absorbent kitchen paper then rub with salt inside and out and leave for about 20 minutes. Pat dry with absorbent kitchen paper.

Set a steamer rack or inverted ramekin in a large wok and pour in enough water to come about 5 cm/2 inches up the side of the wok. Bring to the boil.

Brush a heatproof dinner plate with a little of the groundnut oil and place the fish on the plate with the tails pointing in opposite directions. Place the plate on the rack, cover tightly and simmer over a medium heat for 10–12 minutes, or until tender and the flesh is opaque near the bone. Carefully transfer the plate to a heatproof surface. Sprinkle with the soy sauce and keep warm.

Pour the water out of the wok and return to the heat. Add the remaining groundnut and sesame oils and when hot, add the garlic, ginger and spring onion and stir-fry for 2 minutes, or until golden. Pour over the fish, garnish with chive leaves and lemon slices and serve immediately with rice and an Oriental salad.

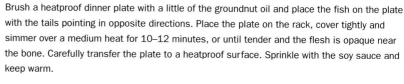

*Try this:* FOR AN ALTERNATIVE: 84 FOR A LIGHT BITE: 74

# Stir–fried Squid with Asparagus

**SERVES 4**

450 g/1 lb squid, cleaned and cut into 1 cm/ ½ inch rings
225 g/8 oz fresh asparagus, sliced diagonally into 6.5 cm/2½ inch pieces
2 tbsp groundnut oil
2 garlic cloves, peeled and thinly sliced
2.5 cm/1 inch piece fresh root ginger, peeled and thinly sliced
225 g/8 oz pak choi, trimmed
75 ml/3 fl oz chicken stock
2 tbsp soy sauce
2 tbsp oyster sauce
1 tbsp Chinese rice wine or dry sherry
2 tsp cornflour, blended with 1 tbsp water
1 tbsp sesame oil
1 tbsp toasted sesame seeds
freshly cooked rice, to serve

Bring a medium saucepan of water to the boil over a high heat. Add the squid, return to the boil and cook for 30 seconds. Using a wide wok strainer or slotted spoon, transfer to a colander, drain and reserve.

Add the asparagus pieces to the boiling water and blanch for 2 minutes. Drain and reserve.

Heat a wok or large frying pan, add the groundnut oil and when hot, add the garlic and ginger and stir-fry for 30 seconds. Add the pak choi, stir-fry for 1–2 minutes, then pour in the stock and cook for 1 minute.

Blend the soy sauce, oyster sauce and Chinese rice wine or sherry in a bowl or jug, then pour into the wok.

Add the reserved squid and asparagus to the wok and stir-fry for 1 minute. Stir the blended cornflour into the wok. Stir-fry for 1 minute, or until the sauce thickens and all the ingredients are well coated. Stir in the sesame oil, give a final stir and turn into a warmed serving dish. Sprinkle with the toasted sesame seeds and serve immediately with freshly cooked rice.

*Try this:* FOR AN ALTERNATIVE: 122 FOR A LIGHT BITE: 46

# Chinese Five Spice Marinated Salmon

**SERVES 4**

700 g/1½ lb skinless salmon fillet, cut into 2.5 cm/1 inch strips
2 medium egg whites
1 tbsp cornflour
vegetable oil for frying
4 spring onions, cut diagonally into
5 cm/2 inch pieces
125 ml/4 fl oz fish stock
lime or lemon wedges, to garnish

**For the marinade:**
3 tbsp soy sauce
3 tbsp Chinese rice wine or dry sherry
2 tsp sesame oil
1 tbsp soft brown sugar
1 tbsp lime or lemon juice
1 tsp Chinese five spice powder
2–3 dashes hot pepper sauce

Combine the marinade ingredients in a shallow nonmetallic baking dish until well blended. Add the salmon strips and stir gently to coat. Leave to marinate in the refrigerator for 20–30 minutes.

Using a slotted spoon or fish slice, remove the salmon pieces, drain on absorbent kitchen paper and pat dry. Reserve the marinade. Beat the egg whites with the cornflour to make a batter. Add the salmon strips and stir into the batter until coated completely.

Pour enough oil into a large wok to come 5 cm/2 inches up the side and place over a high heat. Working in 2 or 3 batches, add the salmon strips and cook for 1–2 minutes or until golden. Remove from the wok with a slotted spoon and drain on absorbent kitchen paper. Reserve.

Discard the hot oil and wipe the wok clean. Add the marinade, spring onions and stock to the wok. Bring to the boil and simmer for 1 minute. Add the salmon strips and stir-fry gently until coated in the sauce. Spoon into a warmed shallow serving dish, garnish with the lime or lemon wedges and serve immediately.

*Try this:* FOR AN ALTERNATIVE: 130 FOR A LIGHT BITE: 50

# Scallops with Black Bean Sauce

**SERVES 4**

700 g/1½ lb scallops, with their coral
2 tbsp vegetable oil
2–3 tbsp Chinese fermented black beans, rinsed, drained and coarsely chopped
2 garlic cloves, peeled and finely chopped
4 cm/1½ inch piece fresh root ginger, peeled and finely chopped
4–5 spring onions, thinly sliced diagonally
2–3 tbsp soy sauce
1½ tbsp Chinese rice wine or dry sherry
1–2 tsp sugar
1 tbsp fish stock or water
2–3 dashes hot pepper sauce
1 tbsp sesame oil
freshly cooked noodles, to serve

Pat the scallops dry with absorbent kitchen paper. Carefully separate the orange coral from the scallop. Peel off and discard the membrane and thickish opaque muscle that attaches the coral to the scallop. Cut any large scallops crossways in half, leave the corals whole.

Heat a wok or large frying pan, add the oil and when hot, add the white scallop meat and stir-fry for 2 minutes, or until just beginning to colour on the edges. Using a slotted spoon or spatula, transfer to a plate. Reserve.

Add the black beans, garlic and ginger and stir-fry for 1 minute. Add the spring onions, soy sauce, Chinese rice wine or sherry, sugar, fish stock or water, hot pepper sauce and the corals and stir until mixed.

Return the scallops and juices to the wok and stir-fry gently for 3 minutes, or until the scallops and corals are cooked through. Add a little more stock or water if necessary. Stir in the sesame oil and turn into a heated serving dish. Serve immediately with noodles.

*Try this:* FOR AN ALTERNATIVE: 112 FOR A LIGHT BITE: 52

# Stir-fried Tiger Prawns

**SERVES 4**

75 g/3 oz fine egg
thread noodles
125 g/4 oz broccoli florets
125 g/4 oz baby sweetcorn,
halved
3 tbsp soy sauce
1 tbsp lemon juice
pinch of sugar
1 tsp chilli sauce

1 tsp sesame oil
2 tbsp sunflower oil
450 g/1 lb raw tiger prawns,
peeled, heads and tails
removed, and deveined
2.5 cm/1 inch piece fresh
root ginger, peeled and
cut into sticks
1 garlic clove, peeled

and chopped
1 red chilli, deseeded
and sliced
2 medium eggs, lightly
beaten
227 g can water chestnuts,
drained and sliced

Place the noodles in a large bowl, cover with plenty of boiling water and leave to stand for 5 minutes, or according to packet directions; stir occasionally. Drain and reserve. Blanch the broccoli and sweetcorn in a saucepan of boiling salted water for 2 minutes, then drain and reserve.

Meanwhile, mix together the soy sauce, lemon juice, sugar, chilli sauce and sesame oil in a bowl and reserve.

Heat a large wok, then add the sunflower oil and heat until just smoking. Add the prawns and stir-fry for 2–3 minutes, or until pink on all sides. Using a slotted spoon, transfer the prawns to a plate and reserve. Add the ginger and stir-fry for 30 seconds. Add the garlic and chilli to the wok and cook for a further 30 seconds.

Add the noodles and stir-fry for 3 minutes, until the noodles are crisp. Stir in the prawns, vegetables, eggs and water chestnuts and stir-fry for a further 3 minutes, until the eggs are lightly cooked. Pour over the chilli sauce, stir lightly and serve immediately.

*Try this:* FOR AN ALTERNATIVE: 134 FOR A LIGHT BITE: 38

# Coconut Seafood

**SERVES 4**

2 tbsp groundnut oil
450 g/1 lb raw king
   prawns, peeled
2 bunches spring onions,
   trimmed and
   thickly sliced
1 garlic clove, peeled
   and chopped

2.5 cm/1 inch piece fresh
   root ginger, peeled and
   cut into matchsticks
125 g/4 oz fresh shiitake
   mushrooms, rinsed
   and halved
150 ml/¼ pint dry white wine
200 ml/7 fl oz carton

coconut cream
4 tbsp freshly chopped
   coriander
salt and freshly ground
   black pepper
freshly cooked fragrant
   Thai rice

Heat a large wok, add the oil and heat until it is almost smoking, swirling the oil around the wok to coat the sides. Add the prawns and stir-fry over a high heat for 4-5 minutes, or until browned on all sides. Using a slotted spoon, transfer the prawns to a plate and keep warm in a low oven.

Add the spring onions, garlic and ginger to the wok and stir-fry for 1 minute. Add the mushrooms and stir-fry for a further 3 minutes. Using a slotted spoon, transfer the mushroom mixture to a plate and keep warm in a low oven.

Add the wine and coconut cream to the wok, bring to the boil and boil rapidly for 4 minutes, until reduced slightly.

Return the mushroom mixture and prawns to the wok, bring back to the boil, then simmer for 1 minute, stirring occasionally, until piping hot. Stir in the freshly chopped coriander and season to taste with salt and pepper. Serve immediately with the freshly cooked fragrant Thai rice.

*Try this:* FOR AN ALTERNATIVE: 98 FOR A LIGHT BITE: 40

# Lobster & Prawn Curry

**SERVES 4**

225 g/8 oz cooked lobster
   meat, shelled if
   necessary
225 g/8 oz raw tiger prawns,
   peeled and deveined
2 tbsp groundnut oil
2 bunches spring onions,
   trimmed and thickly sliced

2 garlic cloves, peeled
   and chopped
2.5 cm/1 inch piece fresh
   root ginger, peeled and
   cut into matchsticks
2 tbsp Thai red curry paste
grated zest and juice of
   1 lime

200 ml/7 fl oz coconut cream
salt and freshly ground
   black pepper
3 tbsp freshly chopped
   coriander
freshly cooked Thai fragrant
   rice, to serve

Using a sharp knife, slice the lobster meat thickly. Wash the tiger prawns and pat dry with absorbent kitchen paper. Make a small 1 cm/½ inch cut at the tail end of each prawn and reserve.

Heat a large wok, then add the oil and, when hot, stir-fry the lobster and tiger prawns for 4–6 minutes, or until pink. Using a slotted spoon, transfer to a plate and keep warm in a low oven.

Add the spring onions and stir-fry for 2 minutes, then stir in the garlic and ginger and stir-fry for a further 2 minutes. Add the curry paste and stir-fry for 1 minute.

Pour in the coconut cream, lime zest and juice and the seasoning. Bring to the boil and simmer for 1 minute. Return the prawns and lobster and any juices to the wok and simmer for 2 minutes. Stir in two-thirds of the freshly chopped coriander to the wok mixture, then sprinkle with the remaining coriander and serve immediately.

*Try this:* FOR AN ALTERNATIVE: 86  FOR A LIGHT BITE: 58

# Prawn Fried Rice

**SERVES 4**

knob of butter
4 medium eggs, beaten
4 tbsp groundnut oil
1 bunch spring onions,
    trimmed and finely
    shredded
125 g/4 oz cooked ham, diced

350 g/12 oz large cooked
    prawns, thawed if frozen
    and peeled
125 g/4 oz peas, thawed if
    frozen
450 g/1 lb cooked
    long-grain rice

2 tbsp dark soy sauce
1 tbsp sherry
salt and freshly ground
    black pepper
1 tbsp freshly shredded
    coriander

Heat a wok, lightly grease with the butter and when melted, pour in half the beaten eggs. Cook for 4 minutes, stirring frequently, until the egg has set, forming an omelette. Using a fish slice, lift the omelette from the wok and roll up into a sausage shape. When cool, using a sharp knife, slice the omelette into thin rings, then reserve.

Wipe the wok clean with absorbent kitchen paper and heat it. Add the oil and heat until just smoking. Add the shredded spring onions, the ham, prawns and peas and stir-fry for 2 minutes, or until heated through thoroughly. Add the cooked rice and stir-fry for a further 2 minutes.

Stir in the remaining beaten eggs and stir-fry for 3 minutes, or until the egg has set. Stir in the soy sauce and sherry and season to taste with salt and pepper, then heat until piping hot. Add the omelette rings and gently stir through the mixture, making sure not to break up the omelette rings. Sprinkle with the freshly shredded coriander and serve immediately.

*Try this:* FOR AN ALTERNATIVE: 376 FOR A LIGHT BITE: 74

# Teriyaki Salmon

**SERVES 4**

450 g/1 lb salmon
  fillet, skinned
6 tbsp Japanese
  teriyaki sauce
1 tbsp rice wine vinegar
1 tbsp tomato paste

dash of Tabasco sauce
grated zest of ½ lemon
salt and freshly ground
  black pepper
4 tbsp groundnut oil
1 carrot, peeled and cut

into matchsticks
125 g/4 oz mangetout peas
125 g/4 oz oyster
  mushrooms, wiped

Using a sharp knife, cut the salmon into thick slices and place in a shallow dish. Mix together the teriyaki sauce, rice wine vinegar, tomato paste, Tabasco sauce, lemon zest and seasoning. Spoon the marinade over the salmon, then cover loosely and leave to marinate in the refrigerator for 30 minutes, turning the salmon or spooning the marinade occasionally over the salmon.

Heat a large wok, then add 2 tablespoons of the oil until almost smoking. Stir-fry the carrot for 2 minutes, then add the mangetout peas and stir-fry for a further 2 minutes. Add the oyster mushrooms and stir-fry for 4 minutes, until softened. Using a slotted spoon, transfer the vegetables to 4 warmed serving plates and keep warm.

Remove the salmon from the marinade, reserving both the salmon and marinade. Add the remaining oil to the wok, heat until almost smoking, then cook the salmon for 4–5 minutes, turning once during cooking, or until the fish is just flaking. Add the marinade and heat through for 1 minute. Serve immediately, with the salmon arranged on top of the vegetables and the marinade drizzled over.

*Try this:* FOR AN ALTERNATIVE: 118 FOR A LIGHT BITE: 26

# Oriental Spicy Scallops

**SERVES 6**

12 fresh scallops, trimmed
12 rashers smoked streaky
   bacon, derinded
2 tbsp groundnut oil
1 red onion, peeled and cut
   into wedges
1 red pepper, deseeded

and sliced
1 yellow pepper, deseeded
   and sliced
2 garlic cloves, peeled
   and chopped
½ tsp garam masala
1 tbsp tomato paste

1 tbsp paprika
4 tbsp freshly chopped
   coriander
freshly cooked noodles,
   to serve
Oriental-style salad

Remove the thin black thread from the scallops, rinse lightly and pat dry on absorbent kitchen paper. Wrap each scallop in a bacon rasher. Place on a baking sheet, cover and chill in the refrigerator for 30 minutes.

Meanwhile heat the wok, then add 1 tablespoon of the oil and stir-fry the onion for 3 minutes, or until almost softened. Add the peppers and stir-fry for 5 minutes, stirring occasionally, until browned. Using a slotted spoon, transfer the vegetables to a plate and reserve.

Add the remaining oil to the wok, heat until almost smoking and then add the scallops, seam-side down, and stir-fry for 2–3 minutes. Turn the scallops over and stir-fry for a further 2–3 minutes, until the bacon is crisp and the scallops are almost tender. Add the garlic, garam masala, tomato paste and paprika and stir until the scallops are lightly coated.

Stir in the remaining ingredients with the reserved vegetables. Stir-fry for a further 1–2 minutes or until the vegetables are piping hot. Serve immediately with noodles and an Oriental salad.

*Try this:* FOR AN ALTERNATIVE: 120 FOR A LIGHT BITE: 46

# Crispy Prawn Stir Fry

**SERVES 4**

3 tbsp soy sauce
1 tsp cornflour
pinch of sugar
6 tbsp groundnut oil
450 g/1 lb raw shelled tiger
  prawns, halved
  lengthways

125 g/4 oz carrots, peeled
  and cut into matchsticks
2.5 cm/1 inch piece fresh
  root ginger, peeled and
  cut into matchsticks
125 g/4 oz mangetout peas,
  trimmed and shredded

125 g/4 oz asparagus spears,
  cut into short lengths
125 g/4 oz beansprouts
¼ head Chinese leaves,
  shredded
2 tsp sesame oil

Mix together the soy sauce, cornflour and sugar in a small bowl and reserve.

Heat a large wok, then add 3 tablespoons of the oil and heat until almost smoking. Add the prawns and stir-fry for 4 minutes, or until pink all over. Using a slotted spoon, transfer the prawns to a plate and keep warm in a low oven.

Add the remaining oil to the wok and when just smoking, add the carrots and ginger and stir-fry for 1 minute, or until slightly softened, then add the mangetout peas and stir-fry for a further 1 minute. Add the asparagus and stir-fry for 4 minutes, or until softened.

Add the beansprouts and Chinese leaves and stir-fry for 2 minutes, or until the leaves are slightly wilted. Pour in the soy sauce mixture and return the prawns to the wok. Stir-fry over a medium heat until piping hot, then add the sesame oil, give a final stir and serve immediately.

*Try this:* FOR AN ALTERNATIVE: 122 FOR A LIGHT BITE: 54

# Spicy Cod Rice

**SERVES 4**

1 tbsp plain flour
1 tbsp freshly chopped
  coriander
1 tsp ground cumin
1 tsp ground coriander
550 g/1¼ lb thick-cut cod
  fillet, skinned and cut into
  large chunks

4 tbsp groundnut oil
50 g/2 oz cashew nuts
1 bunch spring onions,
  trimmed and
  diagonally sliced
1 red chilli, deseeded
  and chopped
1 carrot, peeled and cut

into matchsticks
125 g/4 oz frozen peas
450 g/1 lb cooked
  long-grain rice
2 tbsp sweet chilli sauce
2 tbsp soy sauce

Mix together the flour, coriander, cumin and ground coriander on a large plate. Coat the cod in the spice mixture then place on a baking sheet, cover and chill in the refrigerator for 30 minutes.

Heat a large wok, then add 2 tablespoons of the oil and heat until almost smoking. Stir-fry the cashew nuts for 1 minute, until browned, then remove and reserve.

Add a further 1 tablespoon of the oil and heat until almost smoking. Add the cod and stir-fry for 2 minutes. Using a fish slice, turn the cod pieces over and cook for a further 2 minutes, until golden. Remove from the wok, place on a warm plate, cover and keep warm.

Add the remaining oil to the wok, heat until almost smoking then stir-fry the spring onions and chilli for 1 minute before adding the carrots and peas and stir-frying for a further 2 minutes. Stir in the rice, chilli sauce, soy sauce and cashew nuts and stir-fry for 3 more minutes. Add the cod, heat for 1 minute, then serve immediately.

*Try this:* FOR AN ALTERNATIVE: 288 FOR A LIGHT BITE: 68

# Creamy Spicy Shellfish

**SERVES 4**

2 tbsp groundnut oil
1 onion, peeled and
    chopped
2.5 cm/1 inch piece fresh
    root ginger, peeled
    and grated
225 g/8 oz queen scallops,
    cleaned and rinsed
1 garlic clove, peeled
    and chopped
2 tsp ground cumin
1 tsp paprika
1 tsp coriander seeds,
    crushed
3 tbsp lemon juice
2 tbsp sherry
300 ml/½ pint fish stock
150 ml/¼ pint double cream
225 g/8 oz peeled prawns
225 g/8 oz cooked mussels,
    shelled
salt and freshly ground
    black pepper
2 tbsp freshly chopped
    coriander

Heat a large wok, then add the oil and when hot, stir-fry the onion and ginger for 2 minutes, or until softened. Add the scallops and stir-fry for 2 minutes, or until the scallops are just cooked. Using a slotted spoon, carefully transfer the scallops to a bowl and keep warm in a low oven.

Stir in the garlic, ground cumin, paprika and crushed coriander seeds and cook for 1 minute, stirring constantly. Pour in the lemon juice, sherry and fish stock and bring to the boil. Boil rapidly until reduced by half and slightly thickened.

Stir in the cream and return the scallops and any scallop juices to the wok. Bring to the boil and simmer for 1 minute. Add the prawns and mussels and heat through until piping hot. Season to taste with salt and pepper. Sprinkle with freshly chopped coriander and serve immediately.

*Try this:* FOR AN ALTERNATIVE: 132 FOR A LIGHT BITE: 56

# Tempura

**SERVES 4**

**For the batter:**
200 g/7 oz plain flour
pinch of bicarbonate of soda
1 medium egg yolk

**For the prawns & vegetables:**
8–12 raw king size prawns

1 carrot, peeled
125 g/4 oz button
  mushrooms, wiped
1 green pepper, deseeded
1 small aubergine, trimmed
1 onion, peeled
125 g/4 oz French beans

125 ml/4 fl oz sesame oil
300 ml/½ pint vegetable oil
  for deep frying

soy sauce, to serve
chilli dipping sauce, to serve

Sift the flour and bicarbonate of soda into a mixing bowl. Blend 450 ml/¾ pint water and the egg yolk together, then gradually whisk into the flour mixture until a smooth batter is formed.

Peel the prawns, leaving the tails intact, de-vein, then rinse lightly and pat dry with absorbent kitchen paper and reserve. Slice the carrot thinly then, using small pastry cutters, cut out fancy shapes. Cut the mushrooms in half, if large, and cut the pepper into chunks. Slice the aubergine, then cut into chunks, together with the onion, and finally trim the French beans.

Pour the sesame oil and the vegetable oil into a large wok and heat to 180˚C/350˚F, or until a small spoonful of the batter dropped into the oil sizzles and cooks on impact.

Dip the prawns and vegetables into the reserved batter (no more than 8 pieces at a time) and stir until lightly coated. Cook for 3 minutes, turning occasionally during cooking, or until evenly golden. Using a slotted spoon, transfer the prawns and vegetables onto absorbent kitchen paper and drain well. Keep warm. Repeat with the remaining ingredients. Serve immediately with soy sauce and chilli dipping sauce.

*Try this:* FOR AN ALTERNATIVE: 312 FOR A LIGHT BITE: 54

# Meat

# Pork Fried Noodles

## SERVES 4

125 g/4 oz dried thread
    egg noodles
125 g/4 oz broccoli florets
4 tbsp groundnut oil
350 g/12 oz pork tenderloin,
    cut into slices
3 tbsp soy sauce
1 tbsp lemon juice
pinch of sugar

1 tsp chilli sauce
1 tbsp sesame oil
2.5 cm/1 inch piece fresh
    root ginger, peeled and
    cut into sticks
1 garlic clove, peeled
    and chopped
1 green chilli, deseeded
    and sliced

125 g/4 oz mangetout,
    halved
2 medium eggs,
    lightly beaten
227 g can water chestnuts,
    drained and sliced
radish rose, to garnish
spring onion tassels,
    to garnish

Place the noodles in a bowl and cover with boiling water. Leave to stand for 20 minutes, stirring occasionally, or until tender. Drain and reserve. Meanwhile, blanch the broccoli in a saucepan of lightly salted boiling water for 2 minutes. Drain, refresh under cold running water and reserve.

Heat a large wok or frying pan, add the groundnut oil and heat until just smoking. Add the pork and stir-fry for 5 minutes, or until browned. Using a slotted spoon, remove the pork slices and reserve.

Mix together the soy sauce, lemon juice, sugar, chilli sauce and sesame oil and reserve.

Add the ginger to the wok and stir-fry for 30 seconds. Add the garlic and chilli and stir-fry for 30 seconds. Add the reserved broccoli and stir-fry for 3 minutes. Stir in the mangetout, pork and reserved noodles with the beaten eggs and water chestnuts and stir-fry for 5 minutes or until heated through. Pour over the reserved chilli sauce, toss well and turn into a warmed serving dish. Garnish and serve immediately.

# Hoisin Pork

**SERVES 4**

1.4 kg/3 lb piece lean belly
   pork, boned
sea salt
2 tsp Chinese five

spice powder
2 garlic cloves, peeled
   and chopped
1 tsp sesame oil

4 tbsp hoisin sauce
1 tbsp clear honey
assorted salad leaves,
   to garnish

Preheat the oven to 200°C/400°F/Gas Mark 6, 15 minutes before cooking. Using a sharp knife, cut the pork skin in a crisscross pattern, making sure not to cut all the way through into the flesh. Rub the salt evenly over the skin and leave to stand for 30 minutes.

Meanwhile, mix together the five spice powder, garlic, sesame oil, hoisin sauce and honey until smooth. Rub the mixture evenly over the pork skin. Place the pork on a plate and chill in the refrigerator to marinate for up to 6 hours.

Place the pork on a wire rack set inside a roasting tin and roast the pork in the preheated oven for 1–1¼ hours, or until the pork is very crisp and the juices run clear when pierced with a skewer.

Remove the pork from the heat, leave to rest for 15 minutes, then cut into strips. Arrange on a warmed serving platter. Garnish with salad leaves and serve immediately.

# Coconut Beef

## SERVES 4

450 g/1 lb beef rump or
    sirloin steak
4 tbsp groundnut oil
2 bunches spring onions,
    trimmed and thickly sliced
1 red chilli, deseeded
    and chopped

1 garlic clove, peeled
    and chopped
2 cm/1 inch piece fresh root
    ginger, peeled and cut
    into matchsticks
125 g/4 oz shiitake
    mushrooms

200 ml/7 fl oz coconut cream
150 ml/¼ pint chicken stock
4 tbsp freshly chopped
    coriander
salt and freshly ground
    black pepper
freshly cooked rice, to serve

Trim off any fat or gristle from the beef and cut into thin strips. Heat a wok or large frying pan, add 2 tablespoons of the oil and heat until just smoking. Add the beef and cook for 5–8 minutes, turning occasionally, until browned on all sides. Using a slotted spoon, transfer the beef to a plate and keep warm.

Add the remaining oil to the wok and heat until almost smoking. Add the spring onions, chilli, garlic and ginger and cook for 1 minute, stirring occasionally. Add the mushrooms and stir-fry for 3 minutes. Using a slotted spoon, transfer the mushroom mixture to a plate and keep warm.

Return the beef to the wok, pour in the coconut cream and stock. Bring to the boil and simmer for 3–4 minutes, or until the juices are slightly reduced and the beef is just tender.

Return the mushroom mixture to the wok and heat through. Stir in the chopped coriander and season to taste with salt and pepper. Serve immediately with freshly cooked rice.

 *Try this*: FOR AN ALTERNATIVE: 258  FOR A LIGHT BITE: 42

# Pork Meatballs
# with Vegetables

**SERVES 4**

450 g/1 lb pork mince
2 tbsp freshly chopped
    coriander
2 garlic cloves, peeled
    and chopped
1 tbsp light soy sauce
salt and freshly ground
    black pepper
2 tbsp groundnut oil

2 cm/1 inch piece fresh root
    ginger, peeled and cut
    into matchsticks
1 red pepper, deseeded and
    cut into chunks
1 green pepper, deseeded
    and cut into chunks
2 courgettes, trimmed and
    cut into sticks

125 g/4 oz baby sweetcorn,
    halved lengthways
3 tbsp light soy sauce
1 tsp sesame oil
fresh coriander leaves,
    to garnish
freshly cooked noodles,
    to serve

Mix together the pork mince, the chopped coriander, half the garlic and the soy sauce, then season to taste with salt and pepper. Divide into 20 portions and roll into balls. Place on a baking sheet, cover with clingfilm and chill in the refrigerator for at least 30 minutes.

Heat a wok or large frying pan, add the groundnut oil and when hot, add the meatballs and cook for 8–10 minutes, or until the pork balls are browned all over, turning occasionally. Using a slotted spoon, transfer the balls to a plate and keep warm.

Add the ginger and remaining garlic to the wok and stir-fry for 30 seconds. Add the red and green peppers and stir-fry for 5 minutes. Add the courgettes and sweetcorn and stir-fry for 3 minutes.

Return the pork balls to the wok, add the soy sauce and sesame oil and stir-fry for 1 minute, until heated through. Garnish with coriander leaves and serve immediately on a bed of noodles.

*Try this:* FOR AN ALTERNATIVE: 178   FOR A LIGHT BITE: 70

# Spicy Pork

**SERVES 4**

4 tbsp groundnut oil
2.5 cm/1 inch piece fresh
  root ginger, peeled and
  cut into matchsticks
1 garlic clove, peeled
  and chopped
2 medium carrots, peeled
  and cut into matchsticks

1 medium aubergine,
  trimmed and cubed
700 g/1½ lb pork fillet,
  thickly sliced
400 ml/14 fl oz coconut milk
2 tbsp Thai red curry paste
4 tbsp Thai fish sauce
2 tsp caster sugar

227 g can bamboo shoots in
  brine, drained and cut into
  matchsticks
salt, to taste
lime zest, to garnish
freshly cooked rice, to serve

Heat a wok or large frying pan, add 2 tablespoons of the oil and when hot, add the ginger, garlic, carrots and aubergine and stir-fry for 3 minutes. Using a slotted spoon, transfer to a plate and keep warm.

Add the remaining oil to the wok, heat until smoking, then add the pork and stir-fry for 5–8 minutes or until browned all over. Transfer to a plate and keep warm. Wipe the wok clean.

Pour half the coconut milk into the wok, stir in the red curry paste and bring to the boil. Boil rapidly for 4 minutes, stirring occasionally, or until the sauce is reduced by half.

Add the fish sauce and sugar to the wok and bring back to the boil. Return the pork and vegetables to the wok with the bamboo shoots. Return to the boil, then simmer for 4 minutes.

Stir in the remaining coconut milk and season to taste with salt. Simmer for 2 minutes or until heated through. Garnish with lime zest and serve immediately with rice.

*Try this:* FOR AN ALTERNATIVE: 176  FOR A LIGHT BITE: 28

# Pork with Tofu & Coconut

**SERVES 4**

50 g/2 oz unsalted cashew nuts
1 tbsp ground coriander
1 tbsp ground cumin
2 tsp hot chilli powder
2.5 cm/1 inch piece fresh root ginger, peeled and chopped
1 tbsp oyster sauce
4 tbsp groundnut oil

400 ml/14 fl oz coconut milk
175 g/6 oz rice noodles
450 g/1 lb pork tenderloin, thickly sliced
1 red chilli, deseeded and sliced
1 green chilli, deseeded and sliced
1 bunch spring onions, trimmed and thickly sliced

3 tomatoes, roughly chopped
75 g/3 oz tofu, drained
2 tbsp freshly chopped coriander
2 tbsp freshly chopped mint
salt and freshly ground black pepper

Place the cashew nuts, coriander, cumin, chilli powder, ginger and oyster sauce in a food processor and blend until well ground. Heat a wok or large frying pan, add 2 tablespoons of the oil and when hot, add the cashew mixture and stir-fry for 1 minute. Stir in the coconut milk, bring to the boil, then simmer for 1 minute. Pour into a small jug and reserve. Wipe the wok clean.

Meanwhile, place the rice noodles in a bowl, cover with boiling water, leave to stand for 5 minutes, then drain thoroughly.

Reheat the wok, add the remaining oil and when hot, add the pork and stir-fry for 5 minutes or until browned all over. Add the chillies and spring onions and stir-fry for 2 minutes.

Add the tomatoes and tofu to the wok with the noodles and coconut mixture and stir-fry for a further 2 minutes, or until heated through, being careful not to break up the tofu. Sprinkle with the chopped coriander and mint, season to taste with salt and pepper and stir. Tip into a warmed serving dish and serve immediately.

*Try this:* FOR AN ALTERNATIVE: 338 FOR A LIGHT BITE: 44

# Chilli Beef

**SERVES 4**

550 g/1¼ lb beef rump steak
2 tbsp groundnut oil
2 carrots, peeled and cut
   into matchsticks
125 g/4 oz mangetout,
   shredded

125 g/4 oz beansprouts
1 green chilli, deseeded
   and chopped
2 tbsp sesame seeds
freshly cooked rice, to serve

**For the marinade:**
1 garlic clove, peeled
   and chopped
3 tbsp soy sauce
1 tbsp sweet chilli sauce
4 tbsp groundnut oil

Using a sharp knife, trim the beef, discarding any fat or gristle, then cut into thin strips and place in a shallow dish. Combine all the marinade ingredients in a bowl and pour over the beef. Turn the beef in the marinade until coated evenly, cover with clingfilm and leave to marinate in the refrigerator for at least 30 minutes.

Heat a wok or large frying pan, add the groundnut oil and heat until almost smoking, then add the carrots and stir-fry for 3–4 minutes, or until softened. Add the mangetout and stir-fry for a further 1 minute. Using a slotted spoon, transfer the vegetables to a plate and keep warm.

Lift the beef strips from the marinade, shaking to remove excess marinade. Reserve the marinade. Add the beef to the wok and stir-fry for 3 minutes or until browned all over.

Return the stir-fried vegetables to the wok together with the beansprouts, chilli and sesame seeds and cook for 1 minute. Stir in the reserved marinade and stir-fry for 1–2 minutes or until heated through. Tip into a warmed serving dish or spoon on to individual plates and serve immediately with freshly cooked rice.

*Try this:* FOR AN ALTERNATIVE: 188  FOR A LIGHT BITE: 76

# Pork with Black Bean Sauce

**SERVES 4**

700 g/1½ lb pork tenderloin
4 tbsp light soy sauce
2 tbsp groundnut oil
1 garlic clove, peeled
   and chopped
2.5 cm/1 inch piece fresh
   root ginger, peeled and

cut into matchsticks
1 large carrot, peeled
   and sliced
1 red pepper, deseeded
   and sliced
1 green pepper, deseeded
   and sliced

160 g jar black bean sauce
salt
snipped fresh chives,
   to garnish
freshly steamed rice,
   to serve

Using a sharp knife, trim the pork, discarding any fat or sinew and cut into bite-sized chunks. Place in a large shallow dish and spoon over the soy sauce. Turn to coat evenly, cover with clingfilm and leave to marinate for at least 30 minutes. When in the refrigerator ready to use, lift the pork from the marinade, shaking off as much marinade as possible, and pat dry with absorbent kitchen paper. Reserve the marinade.

Heat a wok, add the groundnut oil and when hot, add the chopped garlic and ginger and stir-fry for 30 seconds. Add the carrot and the red and green peppers and stir-fry for 3–4 minutes or until just softened.

Add the pork to the wok and stir-fry for 5–7 minutes, or until browned all over and tender. Pour in the reserved marinade and black bean sauce. Bring to the boil, stirring constantly until well blended, then simmer for 1 minute, until heated through thoroughly. Tip into a warmed serving dish or spoon on to individual plates. Garnish with snipped chives and serve immediately with steamed rice.

*Try this:* FOR AN ALTERNATIVE: 182 FOR A LIGHT BITE: 28

# Pork Spring Rolls

**SERVES 4**

125 g/4 oz pork tenderloin
2 tbsp light soy sauce
225 ml/8 fl oz groundnut oil
1 medium carrot, peeled and
cut into matchsticks
75 g/3 oz button mushrooms,
wiped and sliced

4 spring onions, trimmed
and thinly sliced
75 g/3 oz beansprouts
1 garlic clove, peeled
and chopped
1 tbsp dark soy sauce
12 large sheets filo pastry

folded in half
spring onion curls,
to garnish
Chinese-style dipping sauce,
to serve

Trim the pork, discarding any sinew or fat, and cut into very fine strips. Place in a small bowl, pour over the light soy sauce and stir until well coated. Cover with clingfilm and leave to marinate in the refrigerator for at least 30 minutes.

Heat a wok or large frying pan, add 1 tablespoon of the oil and when hot, add the carrot and mushrooms and stir-fry for 3 minutes or until softened. Add the spring onions, beansprouts and garlic, stir-fry for 2 minutes, then transfer the vegetables to a bowl and reserve.

Drain the pork well, add to the wok and stir-fry for 2–4 minutes or until browned. Add the pork to the vegetables and leave to cool. Stir in the dark soy sauce and mix the filling well.

Lay the folded filo pastry sheets on a work surface. Divide the filling between the sheets, placing it at one end. Brush the filo edges with water, then fold the sides over and roll up.

Heat the remaining oil in a large wok to 180°C/350°F and cook the spring rolls in batches for 2–3 minutes, or until golden, turning the rolls during cooking. Using a slotted spoon, remove and drain on absorbent kitchen paper. Garnish with spring onion curls and serve immediately with a Chinese-style dipping sauce.

*Try this:* FOR AN ALTERNATIVE: 178  FOR A LIGHT BITE: 52

# Special Fried Rice

**SERVES 4**

25 g/1 oz butter
4 medium eggs, beaten
4 tbsp vegetable oil
1 bunch spring onions,
    trimmed and shredded
225 g/8 oz cooked
    ham, diced
125 g/4 oz large cooked

prawns with tails left on
75 g/3 oz peas, thawed
    if frozen
200 g can water chestnuts,
    drained and roughly
    chopped
450 g/1 lb cooked
    long-grain rice

3 tbsp dark soy sauce
1 tbsp dry sherry
2 tbsp freshly chopped
    coriander
salt and freshly ground
    black pepper

Melt the butter in a wok or large frying pan and pour in half the beaten egg. Cook for 4 minutes drawing the edges of the omelette in to allow the uncooked egg to set into a round shape. Using a fish slice, lift the omelette from the wok and roll into a sausage shape. Leave to cool completely then using a sharp knife slice the omelette into rings.

Wipe the wok with absorbent kitchen paper and return to the heat. Add the oil and when hot, add the spring onions, ham, prawns, peas and chopped water chestnuts and stir-fry for 2 minutes. Add the rice and stir-fry for a further 3 minutes.

Add the remaining beaten eggs and stir-fry for 3 minutes, or until the egg has scrambled and set. Stir in the soy sauce, sherry and chopped coriander. Season to taste with salt and pepper and heat through thoroughly. Add the omelette rings and gently stir without breaking up the egg too much. Serve immediately.

*Try this:* FOR AN ALTERNATIVE: 304  FOR A LIGHT BITE: 74

# Beef & Baby Corn Stir Fry

**SERVES 4**

3 tbsp light soy sauce
1 tbsp clear honey, warmed
450 g/1 lb beef rump steak,
    trimmed and thinly sliced
6 tbsp groundnut oil
125 g/4 oz shiitake
    mushrooms, wiped
    and halved
125 g/4 oz beansprouts,
    rinsed

2.5 cm/1 inch piece fresh
    root ginger, peeled and
    cut into matchsticks
125 g/4 oz mangetout,
    halved lengthways
125 g/4 oz broccoli, trimmed
    and cut into florets
1 medium carrot, peeled and
    cut into matchsticks
125 g/4 oz baby sweetcorn

cobs, halved lengthways
¼ head Chinese leaves,
    shredded
1 tbsp chilli sauce
3 tbsp black bean sauce
1 tbsp dry sherry
freshly cooked noodles,
    to serve

Mix together the soy sauce and honey in a shallow dish. Add the sliced beef and turn to coat evenly. Cover with clingfilm and leave to marinate for at least 30 minutes, turning occasionally.

Heat a wok or large frying pan, add 2 tablespoons of the oil and heat until just smoking. Add the mushrooms and stir-fry for 1 minute. Add the bean sprouts and stir-fry for 1 minute. Using a slotted spoon, transfer the mushroom mixture to a plate and keep warm.

Drain the beef, reserving the marinade. Reheat the wok, pour in 2 tablespoons of the oil and heat until smoking. Add the beef and stir-fry for 4 minutes or until browned. Transfer to a plate and keep warm.

Add the remaining oil to the wok and heat until just smoking. Add the ginger, mangetout, broccoli, carrot and the baby sweetcorn with the shredded Chinese leaves and stir-fry for 3 minutes. Stir in the chilli and black bean sauces, the sherry, the reserved marinade and the beef and mushroom mixture. Stir-fry for 2 minutes, then serve immediately with freshly cooked noodles.

*Try this:* FOR AN ALTERNATIVE: 192  FOR A LIGHT BITE: 42

# Sweet-&-Sour Spareribs

**SERVES 4**

1.6 kg/3½ lb pork spareribs
4 tbsp clear honey
1 tbsp Worcestershire sauce
1 tsp Chinese five
   spice powder

4 tbsp soy sauce
2½ tbsp dry sherry
1 tsp chilli sauce
2 garlic cloves, peeled
   and chopped

1½ tbsp tomato purée
1 tsp dry mustard powder
   (optional)
spring onion curls,
   to garnish

Preheat the oven to 200°C/400°F/Gas Mark 6, 15 minutes before cooking. If necessary, place the ribs on a chopping board and using a sharp knife, cut the joint in between the ribs, to form single ribs. Place the ribs in a shallow dish in a single layer.

Spoon the honey, the Worcestershire sauce, Chinese five spice powder with the soy sauce, sherry and chilli sauce into a small saucepan and heat gently, stirring until smooth. Stir in the chopped garlic, the tomato purée and mustard powder, if using.

Pour the honey mixture over ribs and spoon over until the ribs are coated evenly. Cover with clingfilm and leave to marinate overnight in the refrigerator, occasionally spooning the marinade over the ribs.

When ready to cook, remove the ribs from the marinade and place in a shallow roasting tin. Spoon over a little of the marinade and reserve the remainder. Place the spareribs in the preheated oven and cook for 35–40 minutes, or until cooked and the outsides are crisp. Baste occasionally with the reserved marinade during cooking. Garnish with a few spring onion curls and serve immediately, either as a starter or as a meat accompaniment.

# Lamb with Stir-fried Vegetables

**SERVES 4**

550 g/1¼ lb lamb fillet, cut
    into strips
2.5 cm/1 inch piece fresh
    root ginger, peeled and
    cut into matchsticks
2 garlic cloves, peeled
    and chopped
4 tbsp soy sauce
2 tbsp dry sherry

2 tsp cornflour
4 tbsp groundnut oil
75 g/3 oz French beans,
    trimmed and cut in half
2 medium carrots, peeled
    and cut into matchsticks
1 red pepper, deseeded and
    cut into chunks
1 yellow pepper, deseeded

and cut into chunks
225 g can water chestnuts,
    drained and halved
3 tomatoes, chopped
freshly cooked sticky rice
    in banana leaves, to
    serve (optional)

Place the lamb strips in a shallow dish. Mix together the ginger and half the garlic in a small bowl. Pour over the soy sauce and sherry and stir well. Pour over the lamb and stir until coated lightly. Cover with clingfilm and leave to marinate for at least 30 minutes, occasionally spooning the marinade over the lamb.

Using a slotted spoon, lift the lamb from the marinade and place on a plate. Blend the cornflour and the marinade together until smooth and reserve.

Heat a wok or large frying pan, add 2 tablespoons of the oil and when hot, add the remaining garlic, French beans, carrots and peppers and stir-fry or 5 minutes. Using a slotted spoon, transfer the vegetables to a plate and keep warm.

Heat the remaining oil in the wok, add the lamb and stir-fry for 2 minutes or until tender. Return the vegetables to the wok with the water chestnuts, tomatoes and reserved marinade mixture. Bring to the boil then simmer for 1 minute. Serve immediately with freshly cooked sticky rice in banana leaves, if liked.

*Try this:* FOR AN ALTERNATIVE: 164   FOR A LIGHT BITE: 42

# Szechuan Beef

**SERVES 4**

450 g/1 lb beef fillet
3 tbsp hoisin sauce
2 tbsp yellow bean sauce
2 tbsp dry sherry
1 tbsp brandy
2 tbsp groundnut oil
2 red chillies, deseeded
and sliced
8 bunches spring onions,
trimmed and chopped

2 garlic cloves, peeled
and chopped
2.5 cm/1 inch piece fresh
root ginger, peeled and
cut into matchsticks
1 carrot, peeled, sliced
lengthways and cut into
short lengths
2 green peppers, deseeded
and cut into 2.5 cm/

1 inch pieces
227 g can water chestnuts,
drained and halved
sprigs of fresh coriander,
to garnish
freshly cooked noodles with
freshly ground Szechuan
peppercorns, to serve

Trim the beef, discarding any sinew or fat, then cut into 5 mm/¼ inch strips. Place in a large shallow dish. In a bowl, stir the hoisin sauce, yellow bean sauce, sherry and brandy together until well blended. Pour over the beef and turn until coated evenly. Cover with clingfilm and leave to marinate for at least 30 minutes.

Heat a wok or large frying pan, add the oil and when hot, add the chillies, spring onions, garlic and ginger and stir-fry for 2 minutes or until softened. Using a slotted spoon, transfer to a plate and keep warm.

Add the carrot and peppers to the wok and stir-fry for 4 minutes or until slightly softened. Transfer to a plate and keep warm.

Drain the beef, reserving the marinade, add to the wok and stir-fry for 3–5 minutes or until browned. Return the chilli mixture, the carrot and pepper mixture and the marinade to the wok, add the water chestnuts and stir-fry for 2 minutes or until heated through. Garnish with sprigs of coriander and serve immediately with the noodles.

*Try this:* FOR AN ALTERNATIVE: 196  FOR A LIGHT BITE: 76

# Cashew & Pork Stir Fry

**SERVES 4**

450 g/1 lb pork tenderloin
4 tbsp soy sauce
1 tbsp cornflour
125 g/4 oz unsalted
  cashew nuts
4 tbsp sunflower oil
450 g/1 lb leeks, trimmed

and shredded
2.5 cm/1 inch piece fresh
  root ginger, peeled and
  cut into matchsticks
2 garlic cloves, peeled
  and chopped
1 red pepper, deseeded

and sliced
300 ml/½ pint chicken stock
2 tbsp freshly chopped
  coriander
freshly cooked noodles,
  to serve

Using a sharp knife, trim the pork, discarding any sinew or fat. Cut into 2 cm/¾inch slices and place in a shallow dish. Blend the soy sauce and cornflour together until smooth and free from lumps, then pour over the pork. Stir until coated in the cornflour mixture, then cover with clingfilm and leave to marinate in the refrigerator for at least 30 minutes.

Heat a nonstick frying pan until hot, add the cashew nuts and dry-fry for 2–3 minutes, or until toasted, stirring frequently. Transfer to a plate and reserve.

Heat a wok or large frying pan, add 2 tablespoons of the oil and when hot, add the leeks, ginger, garlic and pepper and stir-fry for 5 minutes or until softened. Using a slotted spoon, transfer to a plate and keep warm.

Drain the pork, reserving the marinade. Add the remaining oil to the wok and when hot, add the pork and stir-fry for 5 minutes or until browned. Return the reserved vegetables to the wok with the marinade and the stock. Bring to the boil, then simmer for 2 minutes, or until the sauce has thickened. Stir in the toasted cashew nuts and chopped coriander and serve immediately with freshly cooked noodles.

*Try this:* FOR AN ALTERNATIVE: 184 FOR A LIGHT BITE: 28

# Barbecued Pork Fillet

**SERVES 4**

2 tbsp clear honey
2 tbsp hoisin sauce
2 tsp tomato purée
2.5 cm/1 inch piece fresh
  root ginger, peeled
  and chopped
450 g/1 lb pork tenderloin
3 tbsp vegetable oil

1 garlic clove, peeled
  and chopped
1 bunch spring onions,
  trimmed and chopped
1 red pepper, deseeded and
  cut into chunks
1 yellow pepper, deseeded
  and cut into chunks

350 g/12 oz cooked
  long-grain rice
125 g/4 oz frozen peas,
  thawed
2 tbsp light soy sauce
1 tbsp sesame oil
50 g/2 oz toasted flaked
  almonds

Preheat the oven to 200°C/400°F/Gas Mark 6, 15 minutes before cooking. Mix together the honey, hoisin sauce, tomato purée and ginger in a bowl. Trim the pork, discarding any sinew or fat. Place in a shallow dish and spread the honey and hoisin sauce over the pork to cover completely. Cover with clingfilm and chill in the refrigerator for 4 hours, turning occasionally.

Remove the pork from the marinade and place in a roasting tin, reserving the marinade. Cook in the preheated oven for 20–25 minutes, or until the pork is tender and the juices run clear when pierced with a skewer. Baste occasionally during cooking with the reserved marinade. Remove the pork from the oven, leave to rest for 5 minutes, then slice thinly and keep warm.

Meanwhile, heat a wok or large frying pan, add the vegetable oil and when hot, add the garlic, spring onions and peppers and stir-fry for 4 minutes or until softened. Add the rice and peas and stir-fry for 2 minutes.

Add the soy sauce, sesame oil and flaked almonds and stir-fry for 30 seconds or until heated through. Tip into a warmed serving dish and top with the sliced pork. Serve immediately.

*Try this:* FOR AN ALTERNATIVE: 190 FOR A LIGHT BITE: 70

# Spicy Lamb & Peppers

**SERVES 4**

550 g/1¼ lb lamb fillet
4 tbsp soy sauce
1 tbsp dry sherry
1 tbsp cornflour
3 tbsp vegetable oil
1 bunch spring onions,
　shredded
225 g/8 oz broccoli florets
2 garlic cloves, peeled

and chopped
2.5 cm/1 inch piece fresh
　root ginger, peeled and
　cut into matchsticks
1 red pepper, deseeded and
　cut into chunks
1 green pepper, deseeded
　and cut into chunks
2 tsp Chinese five

spice powder
1–2 tsp dried crushed
　chillies, or to taste
1 tbsp tomato purée
1 tbsp rice wine vinegar
1 tbsp soft brown sugar
freshly cooked noodles,
　to serve

Cut the lamb into 2 cm/¾ inch slices, then place in a shallow dish. Blend the soy sauce, sherry and cornflour together in a small bowl and pour over the lamb. Turn the lamb until coated lightly with the marinade. Cover with clingfilm and leave to marinate in the refrigerator for at least 30 minutes, turning occasionally.

Heat a wok or large frying pan, add the oil and when hot, stir-fry the spring onions and broccoli for 2 minutes. Add the garlic, ginger and peppers and stir-fry for a further 2 minutes. Using a slotted spoon, transfer the vegetables to a plate and keep warm.

Using a slotted spoon, lift the lamb from the marinade, shaking off any excess marinade. Add to the wok and stir-fry for 5 minutes, or until browned all over. Reserve the marinade.

Return the vegetables to the wok and stir in the Chinese five spice powder, chillies, tomato purée, reserved marinade, vinegar and sugar. Bring to the boil, stirring constantly, until thickened. Simmer for 2 minutes or until heated through thoroughly. Serve immediately with noodles.

# Pork Cabbage Parcels

**SERVES 4**

8 large green cabbage
   leaves
1 tbsp vegetable oil
2 celery sticks, trimmed
   and chopped
1 carrot, peeled and cut
   into matchsticks
125 g/4 oz fresh pork mince
50 g/2 oz button

mushrooms, wiped
   and sliced
1 tsp Chinese five spice
   powder
50 g/2 oz cooked long-
   grain rice
juice of 1 lemon
1 tbsp soy sauce
150 ml/¼ pint chicken stock

**For the tomato sauce:**
1 tbsp vegetable oil
1 bunch spring onions,
   trimmed and chopped
400 g can chopped tomatoes
1 tbsp light soy sauce
1 tbsp freshly chopped mint
freshly ground black pepper

Preheat the oven to 180°C/350°F/Gas Mark 4, 10 minutes before cooking. To make the sauce, heat the oil in a heavy-based saucepan, add the spring onions and cook for 2 minutes or until softened.

Add the tomatoes, soy sauce and mint to the saucepan, bring to the boil, cover, then simmer for 10 minutes. Season to taste with pepper. Reheat when required.

Meanwhile, blanch the cabbage leaves in a large saucepan of lightly salted water for 3 minutes. Drain and refresh under cold running water. Pat dry with absorbent kitchen paper and reserve. Heat the oil in a small saucepan, add the celery, carrot and pork mince and cook for 3 minutes. Add the mushrooms and cook for 3 minutes. Stir in the Chinese five spice powder, rice, lemon juice and soy sauce and heat through.

Place some of the filling in the centre of each cabbage leaf and fold to enclose the filling. Place in a shallow ovenproof dish seam-side down. Pour over the stock and cook in the preheated oven for 30 minutes. Serve immediately with the reheated tomato sauce.

*Try this:* FOR AN ALTERNATIVE: 346  FOR A LIGHT BITE: 70

# Crispy Pork with Tangy Sauce

**SERVES 4**

350 g/12 oz pork fillet
1 tbsp light soy sauce
1 tbsp dry sherry
salt and freshly ground
    black pepper
1 tbsp sherry vinegar

1 tbsp tomato paste
1 tbsp dark soy sauce
2 tsp light muscovado sugar
150 ml/¼ pint chicken stock
1½ tsp clear honey
8 tsp cornflour

450 ml/¾ pint groundnut oil
    for frying
1 medium egg
fresh sprigs of dill,
    to garnish
orange wedges, to garnish

Remove and discard any fat and sinew from the pork fillet, then cut into 2 cm/¾ inch cubes and place in a shallow dish. Blend the light soy sauce with the dry sherry and add seasoning. Pour over the pork and stir until the pork is lightly coated. Cover and leave to marinate in the refrigerator for at least 30 minutes, stirring occasionally.

Meanwhile, blend the sherry vinegar, tomato paste, dark soy sauce, light muscovado sugar, chicken stock and honey together in a small saucepan and heat gently, stirring occasionally, until the sugar has dissolved. Then bring to the boil.

Blend 2 teaspoons of cornflour with 1 tablespoon of water and stir into the sauce. Cook, stirring, until smooth and thickened, and either keep warm or reheat when required.

Heat the oil in the wok to 190˚C/375˚F. Whisk together the remaining 6 teaspoons of cornflour and the egg to make a smooth batter. Drain the pork if necessary, then dip the pieces into the batter, allowing any excess to drip back into the bowl. Cook in the hot oil for 2–3 minutes, or until golden and tender. Drain on kitchen paper. Cook the pork in batches until it is all cooked, then garnish and serve immediately with the sauce.

# Speedy Pork with Yellow Bean Sauce

**SERVES 4**

450 g/1 lb pork fillet
2 tbsp light soy sauce
2 tbsp orange juice
2 tsp cornflour
3 tbsp groundnut oil
2 garlic cloves, peeled
  and crushed

175 g/6 oz carrots, peeled
  and cut into matchsticks
125 g/4 oz fine green beans,
  trimmed and halved
2 spring onions, trimmed
  and cut into strips
4 tbsp yellow bean sauce

1 tbsp freshly chopped flat
  leaf parsley, to garnish
freshly cooked egg noodles,
  to serve

Remove any fat or sinew from the pork fillet, and cut into thin strips. Blend the soy sauce, orange juice and cornflour in a bowl and mix thoroughly. Place the meat in a shallow dish, pour over the soy sauce mixture, cover and leave to marinate in the refrigerator for 1 hour. Drain with a slotted spoon, reserving the marinade.

Heat the wok, then add 2 tablespoons of the oil and stir-fry the pork with the garlic for 2 minutes, or until the meat is sealed. Remove with a slotted spoon and reserve.

Add the remaining oil to the wok and cook the carrots, beans and spring onions for about 3 minutes, until tender but still crisp. Return the pork to the wok with the reserved marinade, then pour over the yellow bean sauce. Stir-fry for a further 1–2 minutes, or until the pork is tender. Sprinkle with the chopped parsley and serve immediately with freshly cooked egg noodles.

*Try this:* FOR AN ALTERNATIVE: 158 FOR A LIGHT BITE: 76

# Honey Pork with Rice Noodles & Cashews

**SERVES 4**

125 g/4 oz rice noodles
450 g/1 lb pork fillet
2 tbsp groundnut oil
1 tbsp softened butter
1 onion, peeled and finely sliced into rings
2 garlic cloves, peeled and crushed
125 g/4 oz baby button mushrooms, halved
3 tbsp light soy sauce
3 tbsp clear honey
50 g/2 oz unsalted cashew nuts
1 red chilli, deseeded and finely chopped
4 spring onions, trimmed and finely chopped
freshly stir-fried vegetables, to serve

Soak the rice noodles in boiling water for 4 minutes or according to packet instructions, then drain and reserve.

Trim and slice the pork fillet into thin strips. Heat the wok, pour in the oil and butter, and stir-fry the pork for 4–5 minutes, until cooked. Remove with a slotted spoon and keep warm.

Add the onion to the wok and stir-fry gently for 2 minutes. Stir in the garlic and mushrooms and cook for a further 2 minutes, or until juices start to run from the mushrooms.

Blend the soy sauce with the honey then return the pork to the wok with this mixture. Add the cashew nuts and cook for 1–2 minutes, then add the rice noodles a little at a time. Stir-fry until everything is piping hot. Sprinkle with chopped chilli and spring onions. Serve immediately with freshly stir-fried vegetables.

*Try this:* FOR AN ALTERNATIVE: 144 FOR A LIGHT BITE: 44

# Sweet-&-Sour Pork

**SERVES 4**

450 g/1 lb pork fillet
1 medium egg white
4 tsp cornflour
salt and freshly ground
    black pepper
300 ml/½ pint groundnut oil
1 small onion, peeled and
    finely sliced

125 g/4 oz carrots, peeled
    and cut into matchsticks
2.5 cm/1 inch piece fresh
    root ginger, peeled and
    cut into thin strips
150 ml/¼ pint orange juice
150 ml/¼ pint chicken stock
1 tbsp light soy sauce

220 g can pineapple
    pieces, drained with
    juice reserved
1 tbsp white wine vinegar
1 tbsp freshly chopped
    parsley
freshly cooked rice, to serve

Trim, then cut the pork fillet into small cubes. In a bowl, whisk the egg white and cornflour with a little seasoning, then add the pork to the egg white mixture and stir until the cubes are well coated.

Heat the wok, then add the oil and heat until very hot before adding the pork and stir-frying for 30 seconds. Turn off the heat and continue to stir for 3 minutes. The meat should be white and sealed. Drain off the oil, reserve the pork and wipe the wok clean.

Pour 2 teaspoons of the drained groundnut oil back into the wok and cook the onion, carrots and ginger for 2–3 minutes. Blend the orange juice with the chicken stock and soy sauce and make up to 300 ml/½ pint with the reserved pineapple juice.

Return the pork to the wok with the juice mixture and simmer for 3–4 minutes. Then stir in the pineapple pieces and vinegar. Heat through, then sprinkle with the chopped parsley and serve immediately with freshly cooked rice.

*Try this:* FOR AN ALTERNATIVE: 166 FOR A LIGHT BITE: 70

# Chilli Lamb

**SERVES 4**

550 g/1¼ lb lamb fillet
3 tbsp groundnut oil
1 large onion, peeled and
    finely sliced
2 garlic cloves, peeled
    and crushed

4 tsp cornflour
4 tbsp hot chilli sauce
2 tbsp white wine vinegar
4 tsp dark soft brown sugar
1 tsp Chinese five
    spice powder

sprigs of fresh coriander,
    to garnish
freshly cooked noodles,
    to serve
4 tbsp Greek style yogurt,
    to serve

Trim the lamb fillet, discarding any fat or sinew, then place it on a clean chopping board and cut into thin strips. Heat a wok and pour in 2 tablespoons of the groundnut oil and when hot, stir-fry the lamb for 3–4 minutes, or until it is browned. Remove the lamb strips with their juices and reserve.

Add the remaining oil to the wok, then stir-fry the onion and garlic for 2 minutes, or until softened. Remove with a slotted spoon and add to the lamb.

Blend the cornflour with 125 ml/4 fl oz of cold water, then stir in the chilli sauce, vinegar, sugar and Chinese five spice powder. Pour this into the wok, turn up the heat and bring the mixture to the boil. Cook for 30 seconds or until the sauce thickens.

Return the lamb to the wok with the onion and garlic, stir thoroughly and heat through until piping hot. Garnish with sprigs of fresh coriander and serve immediately with freshly cooked noodles, topped with a spoonful of Greek yogurt.

*Try this:* FOR AN ALTERNATIVE: 156 FOR A LIGHT BITE: 32

# Pork in Peanut Sauce

**SERVES 4**

450 g/1 lb pork fillet
2 tbsp light soy sauce
1 tbsp vinegar
1 tsp sugar
1 tsp Chinese five
  spice powder
2–4 garlic cloves, peeled
  and crushed

2 tbsp groundnut oil
1 large onion, peeled and
  finely sliced
125 g/4 oz carrots, peeled
  and cut into matchsticks
2 celery sticks, trimmed
  and sliced
125 g/4 oz French beans,

  trimmed and halved
3 tbsp smooth peanut butter
1 tbsp freshly chopped flat
  leaf parsley
freshly cooked basmati and
  wild rice, to serve
green salad, to serve

Remove any fat or sinew from the pork fillet, cut into thin strips and reserve. Blend the soy sauce, vinegar, sugar, Chinese five spice powder and garlic in a bowl and add the pork. Cover and leave to marinate in the refrigerator for at least 30 minutes.

Drain the pork, reserving any marinade. Heat the wok, then add the oil and, when hot, stir-fry the pork for 3–4 minutes, or until sealed.

Add the onion, carrots, celery and beans to the wok and stir-fry for 4–5 minutes, or until the meat is tender and the vegetables are softened.

Blend the reserved marinade, the peanut butter and 2 tablespoons of hot water together. When smooth, stir into the wok and cook for several minutes more until the sauce is thick and the pork is piping hot. Sprinkle with the chopped parsley and serve immediately with the basmati and wild rice and a green salad.

*Try this:* FOR AN ALTERNATIVE: 172 FOR A LIGHT BITE: 32

# Stir-fried Beef with Vermouth

**SERVES 4**

350 g/12 oz beef steak,
   such as rump or sirloin
2 tbsp plain flour
salt and freshly ground
   black pepper
3 tbsp sunflower oil

2 shallots, peeled and
   finely chopped
125 g/4 oz button
   mushrooms, wiped
   and halved
2 tbsp freshly chopped

tarragon
3 tbsp dry vermouth
150 ml/¼ pint single cream
125 g/4 oz stir-fry noodles
2 tsp sesame oil

Trim the beef and cut into thin strips. Place the flour in a bowl and add salt and pepper to taste, then stir well. Add the beef and stir until well coated, then remove from the flour and reserve.

Heat a wok, then add the oil and when hot, add the shallots and stir-fry for 2 minutes. Add the beef strips and stir-fry for 3–4 minutes before adding the mushrooms and 1 tablespoon of the chopped tarragon. Stir-fry for a further 1 minute.

Pour in the vermouth or Martini, stirring continuously, then add the cream. Cook for 2–3 minutes, or until the sauce is slightly thickened and the meat is cooked thoroughly. Adjust the seasoning and keep warm.

Meanwhile, place the noodles in a saucepan and cover with boiling water. Leave to stand for 4 minutes, then drain thoroughly and return to the wok. Add the sesame oil to the noodles and stir-fry for 1–2 minutes, or until heated through thoroughly. Pile the noodles onto serving dishes, top with the beef and serve immediately.

*Try this:* FOR AN ALTERNATIVE: 202 FOR A LIGHT BITE: 28

# Pork with Spring Vegetables & Sweet Chilli Sauce

**SERVES 4**

450 g/16 oz pork fillet
2 tbsp sunflower oil
2 garlic cloves, peeled
and crushed
2.5 cm/1 inch piece fresh
root ginger, peeled
and grated

125 g/4 oz carrots, peeled
and cut into matchsticks
4 spring onions, trimmed
125 g/4 oz sugar snap peas
125 g/4 oz baby sweetcorn
2 tbsp sweet chilli sauce
2 tbsp light soy sauce

1 tbsp vinegar
½ tsp sugar, or to taste
125 g/4 oz beansprouts
grated zest of 1 orange
freshly cooked rice, to serve

Trim, then cut the pork fillet into thin strips and reserve. Heat a wok and pour in the oil. When hot, add the garlic and ginger and stir-fry for 30 seconds. Add the carrots to the wok and continue to stir-fry for 1–2 minute, or until they start to soften.

Slice the spring onions lengthways, then cut into 3 lengths. Trim the sugar snap peas and the sweetcorn. Add the spring onions, sugar snap peas and sweetcorn to the wok and stir-fry for 30 seconds.

Add the pork to the wok and continue to stir-fry for 2–3 minutes, or until the meat is sealed and browned all over. Blend the sweet chilli sauce, soy sauce, vinegar and sugar together, then stir into the wok with the beansprouts.

Continue to stir-fry until the meat is cooked and the vegetables are tender but still crisp. Sprinkle with the orange zest and serve immediately with the freshly cooked rice.

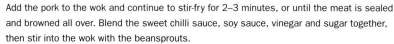

*Try this:* FOR AN ALTERNATIVE: 186  FOR A LIGHT BITE: 54

# Beef with Paprika

## SERVES 4

| | | |
|---|---|---|
| 700 g/1½ lb rump steak | 75 g/3 oz butter | 2 tsp dry sherry |
| 3 tbsp plain flour | 1 tsp oil | 150 ml/¼ pint soured cream |
| salt and freshly ground black pepper | 1 onion, peeled and thinly sliced into rings | 2 tbsp freshly snipped chives |
| 1 tbsp paprika | 225 g/8 oz button mushrooms, wiped and sliced | bundle of chives, to garnish |
| 350 g/12 oz long-grain rice | | |

Beat the steak until very thin, then trim off and discard the fat and cut into thin strips. Season the flour with the salt, pepper and paprika, then toss the steak in the flour until coated.

Meanwhile, place the rice in a saucepan of boiling salted water and simmer for 15 minutes until tender or according to packet directions. Drain the rice, then return to the saucepan, add 25 g/1 oz of the butter, cover and keep warm.

Heat the wok, then add the oil and 25 g/1 oz of the butter. When hot, stir-fry the meat for 3–5 minutes until sealed. Remove from the wok with a slotted spoon and reserve. Add the remaining butter to the wok and stir-fry the onion rings and button mushrooms for 3–4 minutes.

Add the sherry while the wok is very hot, then turn down the heat. Return the steak to the wok with the soured cream and seasoning to taste. Heat through until piping hot, then sprinkle with the snipped chives. Garnish with bundles of chives and serve immediately with the cooked rice.

*Try this:* FOR AN ALTERNATIVE: 198  FOR A LIGHT BITE: 76

# Fried Rice with Chilli Beef

**SERVES 4**

225 g/8 oz beef fillet
375 g/12 oz long-grain rice
4 tbsp groundnut oil
3 onions, peeled and
    thinly sliced

2 hot red chillies, deseeded
    and finely chopped
2 tbsp light soy sauce
2 tsp tomato paste
salt and freshly ground

    black pepper
2 tbsp milk
2 tbsp flour
15 g/ ½ oz butter
2 medium eggs

Trim the beef fillet, discarding any fat, then cut into thin strips and reserve. Cook the rice in boiling salted water for 15 minutes or according to packet directions, then drain and reserve.

Heat a wok and add 3 tablespoons of oil. When hot, add 2 of the sliced onions and stir-fry for 2–3 minutes. Add the beef to the wok, together with the chillies, and stir-fry for a further 3 minutes, or until tender.

Add the rice to the wok with the soy sauce and tomato paste. Stir-fry for 1–2 minutes, or until piping hot. Season to taste with salt and pepper and keep warm. Meanwhile, toss the remaining onion in the milk, then the flour in batches. In a small frying pan fry the onion in the last 1 tablespoon of oil until crisp, then reserve.

Melt the butter in a small omelette pan. Beat the eggs with 2 teaspoons of water and pour into the pan. Cook gently, stirring frequently, until the egg has set, forming an omelette, then slide onto a clean chopping board and cut into thin strips. Add to the fried rice, sprinkle with the crispy onion and serve immediately.

# Shredded Beef in Hoisin Sauce

**SERVES 4**

2 celery sticks
125 g/4 oz carrots
450 g/1 lb rump steak
2 tbsp cornflour
salt and freshly ground
    black pepper

2 tbsp sunflower oil
4 spring onions, trimmed
    and chopped
2 tbsp light soy sauce
1 tbsp hoisin sauce
1 tbsp sweet chilli sauce

2 tbsp dry sherry
250 g pack fine egg
    thread noodles
1 tbsp freshly chopped
    coriander

Trim the celery and peel the carrots, then cut into fine matchsticks and reserve.

Place the steak between 2 sheets of greaseproof paper or baking parchment. Beat the steak with a meat mallet or rolling pin until very thin, then slice into strips. Season the cornflour with salt and pepper and use to coat the steak. Reserve.

Heat a wok, add the oil and when hot, add the spring onions and cook for 1 minute, then add the steak and stir-fry for a further 3–4 minutes, or until the meat is sealed.

Add the celery and carrot matchsticks to the wok and stir-fry for a further 2 minutes before adding the soy, hoisin and chilli sauces and the sherry. Bring to the boil and simmer for 2–3 minutes, or until the steak is tender and the vegetables are cooked.

Plunge the fine egg noodles into boiling water and leave for 4 minutes. Drain, then spoon onto a large serving dish. Top with the cooked shredded steak, then sprinkle with chopped coriander and serve immediately.

*Try this:* FOR AN ALTERNATIVE: 146 FOR A LIGHT BITE: 80

# Beef Curry with Lemon & Arborio Rice

**SERVES 4**

450 g/1 lb beef fillet
1 tbsp olive oil
2 tbsp green curry paste
1 green pepper, deseeded
   and cut into strips
1 red pepper, deseeded

and cut into strips
1 celery stick, trimmed
   and sliced
juice of 1 fresh lemon
2 tsp Thai fish sauce
2 tsp demerara sugar

225 g/8 oz Arborio rice
15 g/ ½ oz butter
2 tbsp freshly chopped
   coriander
4 tbsp crème fraîche

Trim the beef fillet, discarding any fat, then cut across the grain into thin slices. Heat a wok, add the oil and when hot, add the green curry paste and cook for 30 seconds. Add the beef strips and stir-fry for 3–4 minutes.

Add the sliced peppers and the celery and continue to stir-fry for 2 minutes. Add the lemon juice, Thai fish sauce and sugar and cook for a further 3–4 minutes, or until the beef is tender and cooked to personal preference.

Meanwhile, cook the Arborio rice in a saucepan of lightly salted boiling water for i15–20 minutes, or until tender. Drain, rinse with boiling water and drain again. Return to the saucepan and add the butter. Cover and allow the butter to melt before turning it out onto a large serving dish. Sprinkle the cooked curry with the chopped coriander and serve immediately with the rice and crème fraîche.

*Try this:* FOR AN ALTERNATIVE: 214 FOR A LIGHT BITE: 76

# Poultry

# Duck in Black Bean Sauce

**SERVES 4**

450 g/1 lb duck breast,
  skinned
1 tbsp light soy sauce
1 tbsp Chinese rice wine or
  dry sherry
2.5 cm/1 inch piece fresh

root ginger
3 garlic cloves
2 spring onions
2 tbsp Chinese preserved
  black beans
1 tbsp groundnut or

vegetable oil
150 ml/¼ pint chicken stock
shredded spring onions,
  to garnish
freshly cooked noodles,
  to serve

Using a sharp knife, trim the duck breasts, removing any fat. Slice thickly and place in a shallow dish. Mix together the soy sauce and Chinese rice wine or sherry and pour over the duck. Leave to marinate for 1 hour in the refrigerator, then drain and discard the marinade.

Peel the ginger and chop finely. Peel the garlic cloves and either chop finely or crush. Trim the root from the spring onions, discard the outer leaves and chop. Finely chop the black beans.

Heat a wok or large frying pan, add the oil and when very hot, add the ginger, garlic, spring onions and black beans and stir-fry for 30 seconds. Add the drained duck and stir-fry for 3–5 minutes or until the duck is browned.

Add the chicken stock to the wok, bring to the boil, then reduce the heat and simmer for 5 minutes, or until the duck is cooked and the sauce is reduced and thickened. Remove from the heat. Tip on to a bed of freshly cooked noodles, garnish with spring onion shreds and serve immediately.

*Try this:* FOR AN ALTERNATIVE: 244  FOR A LIGHT BITE: 80

# Chinese–glazed Poussin with Green & Black Rice

**SERVES 4**

4 oven-ready poussins
salt and freshly ground
  black pepper
300 ml/½ pint apple juice
1 cinnamon stick
2 star anise
½ tsp Chinese five
  spice powder

50 g/2 oz dark muscovado
  sugar
2 tbsp tomato ketchup
1 tbsp cider vinegar
grated rind of 1 orange
350 g/12 oz mixed basmati
  white and wild rice
125 g/4 oz mangetout, finely

sliced lengthways
1 bunch spring onions,
  trimmed and finely
  shredded lengthways
salt and freshly ground
  black pepper

Preheat the oven to 200°C/400°F/Gas Mark 6, 15 minutes before cooking. Rinse the poussins inside and out and pat dry with absorbent kitchen paper. Using tweezers, remove any feathers. Season well with salt and pepper, then reserve.

Pour the apple juice into a small saucepan and add the cinnamon stick, star anise and spice powder. Bring to the boil, then simmer rapidly until reduced by half. Reduce the heat, stir in the sugar, tomato ketchup, vinegar and orange rind and simmer gently until the sugar is dissolved and the glaze is syrupy. Remove from the heat and leave to cool. Remove the whole spices.

Place the poussins on a wire rack set over a tinfoil-lined roasting tin. Brush generously with the apple glaze. Roast in the preheated oven for 40–45 minutes, or until the juices run clear when the thigh is pierced with a skewer, basting once or twice with the remaining glaze. Remove the poussins from the oven and leave to cool slightly.

Meanwhile, cook the rice according to the packet instructions. Bring a large saucepan of lightly salted water to the boil and add the mangetout. Blanch for 1 minute, then drain thoroughly. As soon as the rice is cooked, drain and transfer to a warmed bowl. Add the mangetout and spring onions, season to taste and stir well. Arrange on warmed dinner plates, place a poussin on top and serve immediately.

# Braised Chicken with Aubergine

**SERVES 4**

3 tbsp vegetable oil
12 chicken thighs
2 large aubergines, trimmed
    and cubed
4 garlic cloves, peeled
    and crushed
2 tsp freshly grated
    root ginger

900 ml/1½ pints
    vegetable stock
2 tbsp light soy sauce
2 tbsp Chinese preserved
    black beans
6 spring onions, trimmed
    and thinly sliced
    diagonally

1 tbsp cornflour
1 tbsp sesame oil
spring onion tassels,
    to garnish
freshly cooked noodles or
    rice, to serve

Heat a wok or large frying pan, add the oil and when hot, add the chicken thighs and cook over a medium high heat for 5 minutes, or until browned all over. Transfer to a large plate and keep warm.

Add the aubergine to the wok and cook over a high heat for 5 minutes or until browned, turning occasionally. Add the garlic and ginger and stir-fry for 1 minute.

Return the chicken to the wok, pour in the stock and add the soy sauce and black beans. Bring to the boil, then simmer for 20 minutes, or until the chicken is tender. Add the spring onions after 10 minutes.

Blend the cornflour with 2 tablespoons of water. Stir into the wok and simmer until the sauce has thickened. Stir in the sesame oil, heat for 30 seconds, then remove from the heat. Garnish with spring onion tassels and serve immediately with noodles or rice.

*Try this:* FOR AN ALTERNATIVE: 220  FOR A LIGHT BITE: 66

# Stir-fried Duck with Cashews

**SERVES 4**

450 g/1 lb duck
   breast, skinned
3 tbsp groundnut oil
1 garlic clove, peeled and
   finely chopped
1 tsp freshly grated
   ginger root

1 carrot, peeled and sliced
125 g/4 oz mangetout,
   trimmed
2 tsp Chinese rice wine or
   dry sherry
1 tbsp light soy sauce
1 tsp cornflour

50 g/2 oz unsalted cashew
   nuts, roasted
1 spring onion, trimmed and
   finely chopped
1 spring onion, shredded
boiled or steamed rice,
   to serve

Trim the duck breasts, discarding any fat and slice thickly. Heat the wok, add 2 tablespoons of the oil and when hot, add the sliced duck breast. Cook for 3–4 minutes or until sealed. Using a slotted spoon, remove from the wok and leave to drain on absorbent kitchen paper.

Wipe the wok clean and return to the heat. Add the remaining oil and when hot, add the garlic and ginger. Stir-fry for 30 seconds, then add the carrot and mangetout. Stir-fry for a further 2 minutes, then pour in the Chinese rice wine or sherry and soy sauce.

Blend the cornflour with 1 teaspoon of water and stir into the wok. Mix well and bring to the boil. Return the duck slices to the wok and simmer for 5 minutes, or until the meat and vegetables are tender. Add the cashews, then remove the wok from the heat.

Sprinkle over the chopped and shredded spring onion and serve immediately with plain boiled or steamed rice.

*Try this:* FOR AN ALTERNATIVE: 262  FOR A LIGHT BITE: 80

# Stir-fried Lemon Chicken

**SERVES 4**

350 g/12 oz boneless, skinless chicken breast
1 large egg white
5 tsp cornflour
3 tbsp vegetable or groundnut oil

150 ml/¼ pint chicken stock
2 tbsp fresh lemon juice
2 tbsp light soy sauce
1 tbsp Chinese rice wine or dry sherry
1 tbsp sugar

2 garlic cloves, peeled and finely chopped
¼ tsp dried chilli flakes, or to taste
lemon rind strips, to garnish
red chilli slices, to garnish

Using a sharp knife, trim the chicken, discarding any fat and cut into thin strips, about 5 cm/2 inch long and 1 cm/½ inch wide. Place in a shallow dish. Lightly whisk the egg white and 1 tablespoon of the cornflour together until smooth. Pour over the chicken strips and mix well until coated evenly. Leave to marinate in the refrigerator for at least 20 minutes.

When ready to cook, drain the chicken and reserve. Heat a wok or large frying pan, add the oil and when hot, add the chicken and stir-fry for 1–2 minutes, or until the chicken has turned white. Using a slotted spoon, remove from the wok and reserve.

Wipe the wok clean and return to the heat. Add the chicken stock, lemon juice, soy sauce, Chinese rice wine or sherry, sugar, garlic and chilli flakes and bring to the boil. Blend the remaining cornflour with 1 tablespoon of water and stir into the stock. Simmer for 1 minute.

Return the chicken to the wok and continue simmering for a further 2–3 minutes, or until the chicken is tender and the sauce has thickened. Garnish with lemon strips and red chilli slices. Serve immediately.

*Try this:* FOR AN ALTERNATIVE: 264   FOR A LIGHT BITE: 20

# Turkey & Vegetable Stir Fry

**SERVES 4**

350 g/12 oz mixed
   vegetables, such as
   baby sweetcorn, 1 small
   red pepper, pak choi,
   mushrooms, broccoli
   florets and baby carrots
1 red chilli
2 tbsp groundnut oil
350 g/12 oz skinless,
   boneless turkey breast,
   sliced into fine strips

across the grain
2 garlic cloves, peeled and
   finely chopped
2.5 cm/1 inch piece fresh
   root ginger, peeled and
   finely grated
3 spring onions, trimmed
   and finely sliced
2 tbsp light soy sauce
1 tbsp Chinese rice wine or
   dry sherry

2 tbsp chicken stock or water
1 tsp cornflour
1 tsp sesame oil
freshly cooked noodles or
   rice, to serve
50 g/2 oz toasted
   cashew nuts, to garnish
2 spring onions, finely
   shredded, to garnish
25 g/1 oz beansprouts,
   to garnish

Slice or chop the vegetables into small pieces, depending on which you use. Halve the baby sweetcorn lengthways, deseed and thinly slice the red pepper, tear or shred the pak choi, slice the mushrooms, break the broccoli into small florets and cut the carrots into matchsticks. Deseed and finely chop the chilli.

Heat a wok or large frying pan, add the oil and when hot, add the turkey and stir-fry for 1 minute or until white. Add the garlic, ginger, spring onions and chilli and cook for a few seconds.

Add the prepared carrot, pepper, broccoli and mushrooms and stir-fry for 1 minute. Add the baby sweetcorn and pak choi and stir-fry for 1 minute.

Blend the soy sauce, Chinese rice wine or sherry and stock or water and pour over the vegetables. Blend the cornflour with 1 teaspoon of water and stir into the vegetables, mixing well. Bring to the boil, reduce the heat, then simmer for 1 minute. Stir in the sesame oil. Tip into a warmed serving dish, sprinkle with cashew nuts, shredded spring onions and beansprouts. Serve immediately with noodles or rice.

*Try this:* FOR AN ALTERNATIVE: 238   FOR A LIGHT BITE: 34

# Crispy Roast Duck Legs with Pancakes

**SERVES 6**

900 g/2 lb plums, halved
25 g/1 oz butter
2 star anise
1 tsp freshly grated
   root ginger
50 g/2 oz soft brown sugar

zest and juice of 1 orange
salt and freshly ground
   black pepper
4 duck legs
3 tbsp dark soy sauce
2 tbsp dark brown sugar

½ cucumber, cut into
   matchsticks
1 small bunch spring onions,
   trimmed and shredded
18 ready-made Chinese
   pancakes, warmed

Preheat the oven to 220°C/425°F/Gas Mark 7, 15 minutes before cooking. Discard stones from plums and place in a saucepan with the butter, star anise, ginger, brown sugar and orange zest and juice. Season to taste with pepper. Cook over a gentle heat until the sugar has dissolved. Bring to the boil, then reduce heat and simmer for 15 minutes, stirring occasionally until the plums are soft and the mixture is thick. Remove the star anise. Leave to cool.

Using a fork, prick the duck legs all over. Place in a large bowl and pour boiling water over to remove some of the fat. Drain, pat dry on absorbent kitchen paper and leave until cold.

Mix together the soy sauce, dark brown sugar and the ½ teaspoon of salt. Rub this mixture generously over the duck legs. Transfer to a wire rack set over a roasting tin and roast in the preheated oven for 30–40 minutes, or until well cooked and the skin is browned and crisp. Remove from the oven and leave to rest for 10 minutes.

Shred the duck meat using a fork to hold the hot duck leg and another to remove the meat. Transfer to a warmed serving platter with the cucumber and spring onions. Serve immediately with the plum compote and warmed pancakes.

*Try this:* FOR AN ALTERNATIVE: 272   FOR A LIGHT BITE: 80

# Chinese Barbecue–style Quails with Aubergines

**SERVES 6**

4 quails
2 tbsp salt
3 tbsp hoisin sauce
1 tbsp Chinese rice wine or
   dry sherry
1 tbsp light soy sauce
700 g/1½ lb aubergines,
   trimmed and cubed

1 tbsp oil
4 garlic cloves, peeled
   and finely chopped
1 tbsp freshly chopped
   root ginger
6 spring onions, trimmed
   and finely chopped
3 tbsp dark soy sauce

¼ tsp dried chilli flakes
1 tbsp yellow bean sauce
1 tbsp sugar
sprigs of fresh coriander,
   to garnish
sliced red chilli, to garnish

Preheat the oven to 240°C/475°F/Gas Mark 9. Rub the quails inside and out with 1 tablespoon of the salt. Mix together the hoisin sauce, Chinese rice wine or sherry and light soy sauce. Rub the quails inside and out with the sauce. Transfer to a small roasting tin and roast in the preheated oven for 5 minutes. Reduce the heat to 180°C/350°F/Gas Mark 4 and continue to roast for 20 minutes. Turn the oven off and leave the quails for 5 minutes, then remove and leave to rest for 10 minutes.

Place the aubergine in a colander and sprinkle with the remaining salt. Leave to drain for 20 minutes, then rinse under cold running water and pat dry with absorbent kitchen paper.

Heat a wok or large frying pan over a moderate heat. Add the oil and when hot, add the aubergines, garlic, ginger and 4 of the spring onions and cook for 1 minute. Add the dark soy sauce, chilli flakes, yellow bean sauce, sugar and 450 ml/¾ pint of water. Bring to the boil, then simmer uncovered for 10–15 minutes. Increase the heat to high and continue to cook, stirring occasionally, until the sauce is reduced and slightly thickened. Spoon the aubergine mixture on to warmed individual plates and top with a quail. Garnish with the remaining spring onion, fresh chilli and a sprig of coriander and serve immediately.

# Chinese Braised White Chicken with Three Sauces

**SERVES 4**

1.4 kg/3 lb oven-ready chicken
salt
6 spring onions, trimmed
5 cm/2 inch piece fresh root
　ginger, peeled and sliced
2 tsp Szechuan peppercorns,
　crushed
2½ tsp sea salt flakes or
　crushed coarse sea salt

2 tsp freshly grated
　root ginger
4 tbsp dark soy sauce
4 tbsp sunflower oil
1 tsp caster sugar
2 garlic cloves, finely chopped
3 tbsp light soy sauce
1 tbsp Chinese rice wine or
　dry sherry

1 tsp sesame oil
3 tbsp rice vinegar
1 small hot red chilli,
　deseeded and finely
　sliced spring onion
　curls, to garnish
freshly steamed
　saffron-flavoured rice,
　to serve

Remove any fat from inside the chicken, rub inside and out with ½ teaspoon of salt and leave for 20 minutes. Place 3.4 litres/6 pints water with 2 spring onions and the ginger in a saucepan and bring to the boil. Add the chicken, breast-side down, return to the boil, cover and simmer for 20 minutes. Remove from the heat and leave for 1 hour. Remove the chicken and leave to cool.

Dry-fry the Szechuan peppercorns in a nonstick frying pan until they darken slightly and smell aromatic. Crush, mix with the sea salt and reserve. Squeeze the juice from half of the grated ginger, mix with the dark soy sauce, 1 tablespoon of the sunflower oil and half the sugar. Reserve.

Finely chop the remaining spring onions and mix with the remaining ginger and garlic in a bowl. Heat the remaining oil to smoking and pour over the onion and ginger. When they stop sizzling, stir in the light soy sauce, Chinese rice wine or sherry and sesame oil. Reserve.

Mix together the rice vinegar, remaining sugar and chilli. Stir until the sugar dissolves. Reserve. Remove the skin from the chicken, then remove the legs and cut them in 2 at the joint. Lift the breast meat away from the carcass in 2 pieces and slice thickly crossways. Sprinkle the pepper and salt mixture over the chicken, garnish with spring onion curls and serve with the dipping sauces, spring onion mixture and rice.

# Orange Roasted Whole Chicken

**SERVES 6**

1 small orange, thinly sliced
50 g/2 oz sugar
1.4 kg/3 lb oven-ready
  chicken
1 small bunch fresh
  coriander

1 small bunch fresh mint
2 tbsp olive oil
1 tsp Chinese five
  spice powder
½ tsp paprika
1 tsp fennel seeds, crushed

salt and freshly ground
  black pepper
sprigs of fresh coriander,
  to garnish
freshly cooked vegetables,
  to serve

Preheat the oven to 190°C/375°F/Gas Mark 5, 10 minutes before cooking. Place the orange slices in a small saucepan, cover with water, bring to the boil, then simmer for 2 minutes and drain. Place the sugar in a clean saucepan with 150 ml/¼ pint fresh water. Stir over a low heat until the sugar dissolves, then bring to the boil, add the drained orange slices and simmer for 10 minutes. Remove from the heat and leave in the syrup until cold.

Remove any excess fat from inside the chicken. Starting at the neck end, carefully loosen the skin of the chicken over the breast and legs without tearing. Push the orange slices under the loosened skin with the coriander and mint.

Mix together the olive oil, Chinese five spice powder, paprika and crushed fennel seeds and season to taste with salt and pepper. Brush the chicken skin generously with this mixture. Transfer to a wire rack set over a roasting tin and roast in the preheated oven for 1½ hours, or until the juices run clear when a skewer is inserted into the thickest part of the thigh. Remove from the oven and leave to rest for 10 minutes. Garnish with sprigs of fresh coriander and serve with freshly cooked vegetables.

*Try this:* FOR AN ALTERNATIVE: 218   FOR A LIGHT BITE: 50

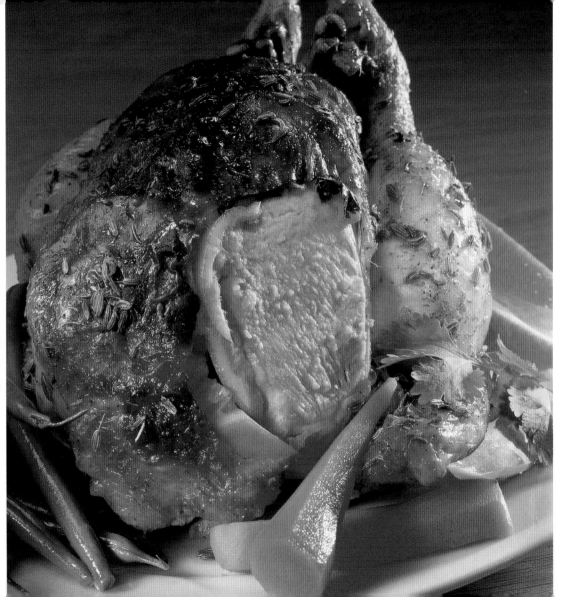

# Baked Thai Chicken Wings

**SERVES 4**

4 tbsp clear honey
1 tbsp chilli sauce
1 garlic clove, peeled and crushed
1 tsp freshly grated root ginger
1 lemon grass stalk, outer leaves discarded and finely chopped
2 tbsp lime zest
3–4 tbsp freshly squeezed lime juice
1 tbsp light soy sauce
1 tsp ground cumin
1 tsp ground coriander
¼ tsp ground cinnamon
1.4 kg/3 lb chicken wings (about 12 large wings)
6 tbsp mayonnaise
2 tbsp freshly chopped coriander
lemon or lime wedges, to garnish

Preheat the oven to 190°C/375°F/Gas Mark 5, 10 minutes before cooking. In a small saucepan, mix together the honey, chilli sauce, garlic, ginger, lemon grass, 1 tablespoon of the lime zest and 2 tablespoons of the lime juice with the soy sauce, cumin, coriander and cinnamon. Heat gently until just starting to bubble, then remove from the heat and leave to cool.

Prepare the chicken wings by folding the tips back under the thickest part of the meat to form a triangle. Arrange in a shallow ovenproof dish. Pour over the honey mixture, turning the wings to ensure that they are all well coated. Cover with clingfilm and leave to marinate in the refrigerator for 4 hours or overnight, turning once or twice.

Mix together the mayonnaise with the remaining lime zest and juice and the coriander. Leave to let the flavours develop while the wings are cooking.

Arrange the wings on a rack set over a tinfoil-lined roasting tin. Roast at the top of the preheated oven for 50–60 minutes, or until the wings are tender and golden, basting once or twice with the remaining marinade and turning once. Remove from the oven. Garnish the wings with lemon or lime wedges and serve immediately with the mayonnaise.

*Try this:* FOR AN ALTERNATIVE: 166  FOR A LIGHT BITE: 78

# Seared Duck with Pickled Plums

**SERVES 4**

4 small skinless, boneless
   duck breasts
2 garlic cloves, peeled
   and crushed
1 tsp hot chilli sauce
2 tsp clear honey
2 tsp dark brown sugar
juice of 1 lime

1 tbsp dark soy sauce
6 large plums, halved and
   stones removed
50 g/2 oz caster sugar
50 ml/2 fl oz white
   wine vinegar
¼ tsp dried chilli flakes
¼ tsp ground cinnamon

1 tbsp sunflower oil
150 ml/¼ pint chicken stock
2 tbsp oyster sauce
sprigs of fresh flat leaf
   parsley, to garnish
freshly cooked noodles,
   to serve

Cut a few deep slashes in each duck breast and place in a shallow dish. Mix together the garlic, chilli sauce, honey, brown sugar, lime juice and soy sauce. Spread over the duck and leave to marinate in the refrigerator for 4 hours or overnight, if time permits, turning occasionally.

Place the plums in a saucepan with the caster sugar, white wine vinegar, chilli flakes and cinnamon and bring to the boil. Simmer gently for 5 minutes, or until the plums have just softened, then leave to cool.

Remove the duck from the marinade and pat dry with absorbent kitchen paper. Reserve the marinade. Heat a wok or large frying pan, add the oil and when hot, brown the duck on both sides. Pour in the stock, oyster sauce and reserved marinade and simmer for 5 minutes. Remove the duck and keep warm.

Remove the plums from their liquid and reserve. Pour the liquid into the duck sauce, bring to the boil, then simmer, uncovered, for 5 minutes, or until reduced and thickened. Arrange the duck on warmed plates. Divide the plums between the plates and spoon over the sauce. Garnish with parsley and serve immediately with noodles.

*Try this:* FOR AN ALTERNATIVE: 272   FOR A LIGHT BITE: 80

# Thai Stuffed Omelette

**SERVES 4**

1 shallot, peeled and
　roughly chopped
1 garlic clove, peeled and
　roughly chopped
1 small red chilli, deseeded
　and roughly chopped
15 g/½ oz coriander leaves
pinch of sugar
2 tsp light soy sauce
2 tsp Thai fish sauce
4 tbsp vegetable or

groundnut oil
175 g/6 oz skinless,
　boneless chicken
　breast, finely sliced
½ small aubergine, trimmed
　and diced
50 g/2 oz button or
　shiitake mushrooms,
　wiped and sliced
½ small red pepper,
　deseeded and sliced

50 g/2 oz fine green beans,
　trimmed and halved
2 spring onions, trimmed
　and thickly sliced
25 g/1 oz peas, thawed
　if frozen
6 medium eggs
salt and freshly ground
　black pepper
sprig of fresh basil,
　to garnish

Place the shallot, garlic, chilli, coriander and sugar in the bowl of a spice grinder or food processor. Blend until finely chopped. Add the soy sauce, fish sauce and 1 tablespoon of the vegetable oil and blend briefly to mix into a paste. Reserve.

Heat a wok or large frying pan, add 1 tablespoon of the oil and when hot, add the chicken and aubergine and stir-fry for 3–4 minutes, or until golden. Add the mushrooms, red pepper, green beans and spring onions and stir-fry for 3–4 minutes or until tender, adding the peas for the final 1 minute. Remove from the heat and stir in the reserved coriander paste. Reserve.

Beat the eggs in a bowl and season to taste with salt and pepper. Heat the remaining oil in a large nonstick frying pan and add the eggs, tilting the pan so that the eggs cover the bottom. Stir the eggs until they are starting to set all over, then cook for 1–2 minutes, or until firm and set on the bottom but still slightly soft on top. Spoon the chicken and vegetable mixture on to one-half of the omelette and carefully flip the other half over. Cook over a low heat for 2–3 minutes, or until the omelette is set and the chicken and vegetables are heated through. Garnish with a sprig of basil and serve immediately.

*Try this:* FOR AN ALTERNATIVE: 334 FOR A LIGHT BITE: 34

# Red Chicken Curry

**SERVES 4**

225 ml/8 fl oz coconut cream
2 tbsp vegetable oil
2 garlic clove, peeled and
   finely chopped
2 tbsp Thai red curry paste
2 tbsp Thai fish sauce

2 tsp sugar
350 g/12 oz boneless,
   skinless chicken breast,
   finely sliced
450 ml/¾ pint chicken stock
2 lime leaves, shredded

chopped red chilli,
   to garnish
freshly boiled rice or
   steamed Thai fragrant
   rice, to serve

Pour the coconut cream into a small saucepan and heat gently. Meanwhile, heat a wok or large frying pan and add the oil. When the oil is very hot, swirl the oil around the wok until the wok is lightly coated, then add the garlic and stir-fry for about 10–20 seconds, or until the garlic begins to brown. Add the curry paste and stir-fry for a few more seconds, then pour in the warmed coconut cream.

Cook the coconut cream mixture for 5 minutes, or until the cream has curdled and thickened. Stir in the fish sauce and sugar. Add the finely sliced chicken breast and cook for 3–4 minutes, or until the chicken has turned white.

Pour the stock into the wok, bring to the boil, then simmer for 1–2 minutes, or until the chicken is cooked through. Stir in the shredded lime leaves. Turn into a warmed serving dish, garnish with chopped red chilli and serve immediately with rice.

*Try this:* FOR AN ALTERNATIVE: 234   FOR A LIGHT BITE: 78

# Green Turkey Curry

**SERVES 4**

4 baby aubergines, trimmed
   and quartered
1 tsp salt
2 tbsp sunflower oil
4 shallots, peeled and
   halved or quartered
   if large
2 garlic cloves, peeled
   and sliced

2 tbsp Thai green curry
   paste
150 ml/¼ pint chicken stock
1 tbsp Thai fish sauce
1 tbsp lemon juice
350 g/12 oz boneless,
   skinless turkey
   breast, cubed
1 red pepper, deseeded

   and sliced
125 g/4 oz French beans,
   trimmed and halved
25 g/1 oz creamed coconut
freshly boiled rice or
   steamed Thai fragrant
   rice, to serve

Place the aubergines into a colander and sprinkle with the salt. Set over a plate or in the sink to drain and leave for 30 minutes. Rinse under cold running water and pat dry on absorbent kitchen paper.

Heat a wok or large frying pan, add the sunflower oil and when hot, add the shallots and garlic and stir-fry for 3 minutes, or until beginning to brown. Add the curry paste and stir-fry for 1–2 minutes. Pour in the stock, fish sauce and lemon juice and simmer for 10 minutes.

Add the turkey, red pepper and French beans to the wok with the aubergines. Return to the boil, then simmer for 10–15 minutes, or until the turkey and vegetables are tender. Add the creamed coconut and stir until melted and the sauce has thickened. Turn into a warmed serving dish and serve immediately with rice.

*Try this:* FOR AN ALTERNATIVE: 246  FOR A LIGHT BITE: 72

# Thai Chicken with Chilli & Peanuts

**SERVES 4**

2 tbsp vegetable or groundnut oil
1 garlic clove, peeled and finely chopped
1 tsp dried chilli flakes
350 g/12 oz boneless, skinless chicken breast, finely sliced
1 tbsp Thai fish sauce
2 tbsp peanuts, roasted and roughly chopped
225 g/ 8 oz sugar snap peas
3 tbsp chicken stock
1 tbsp light soy sauce
1 tbsp dark soy sauce
large pinch of sugar
freshly chopped coriander, to garnish
boiled or steamed rice, to serve

Heat a wok or large frying pan, add the oil and when hot, carefully swirl the oil around the wok until the sides are lightly coated with the oil. Add the garlic and stir-fry for 10–20 seconds, or until starting to brown. Add the chilli flakes and stir-fry for a few seconds more.

Add the finely sliced chicken to the wok and stir-fry for 2–3 minutes, or until the chicken has turned white.

Add the following ingredients, stirring well after each addition: fish sauce, peanuts, sugar snap peas, chicken stock, light and dark soy sauces and sugar. Give a final stir.

Bring the contents of the wok to the boil, then simmer gently for 3–4 minutes, or until the chicken and vegetables are tender. Remove from the heat and tip into a warmed serving dish. Garnish with chopped coriander and serve immediately with boiled or steamed rice.

*Try this:* FOR AN ALTERNATIVE: 190  FOR A LIGHT BITE: 32

# Thai Stir–fried Spicy Turkey

**SERVES 4**

2 tbsp Thai fragrant rice
2 tbsp lemon juice
3–5 tbsp chicken stock
2 tbsp Thai fish sauce
½–1 tsp cayenne pepper, or
   to taste

125 g/4 oz fresh turkey mince
2 shallots, peeled and
   chopped
¼ lemon grass stalk, outer
   leaves discarded and
   finely sliced

1 lime leaf, finely sliced
1 spring onion, trimmed and
   finely chopped
freshly chopped coriander,
   to garnish
Chinese leaves, to serve

Place the rice in a small frying pan and cook, stirring constantly, over a medium high heat for 4–5 minutes, or until the rice is browned. Transfer to a spice grinder or blender and pulse briefly until roughly ground. Reserve.

Place the lemon juice, 3 tablespoons of the stock, the fish sauce and cayenne pepper into a small saucepan and bring to the boil. Add the turkey mince and return to the boil. Continue cooking over a high heat until the turkey is sealed all over.

Add the shallots to the saucepan with the lemon grass, lime leaf, spring onion and reserved rice. Continue cooking for another 1–2 minutes, or until the turkey is cooked through, adding a little more stock, if necessary to keep the mixture moist.

Spoon a little of the mixture into each Chinese leaf and arrange on a serving dish or individual plates. Garnish with a little chopped coriander and serve immediately.

# Hot-&-Sour Duck

**SERVES 4**

4 small boneless duck
  breasts, with skin on,
  thinly sliced on the
  diagonal
1 tsp salt
4 tbsp tamarind pulp
4 shallots, peeled and
  chopped
2 garlic cloves, peeled

and chopped
2.5 cm/1 inch piece fresh
  root ginger, chopped
1 tsp ground coriander
3 large red chillies,
  deseeded and chopped
½ tsp turmeric
6 blanched almonds,
  chopped

125 ml/4 fl oz vegetable oil
227 g can bamboo shoots,
  drained, rinsed and
  finely sliced
salt and freshly ground
  black pepper
sprigs of fresh coriander,
  to garnish
freshly cooked rice, to serve

Sprinkle the duck with the salt, cover lightly and refrigerate for 20 minutes.

Meanwhile, place the tamarind pulp in a small bowl, pour over 4 tablespoons of hot water and leave for 2–3 minutes or until softened. Press the mixture through a sieve into another bowl to produce about 2 tablespoons of smooth juice.

Place the tamarind juice in a food processor with the shallots, garlic, ginger, coriander, chillies, turmeric and almonds. Blend until smooth, adding a little more hot water if necessary, and reserve the paste.

Heat a wok or large frying pan, add the oil and when hot, stir-fry the duck in batches for about 3 minutes, or until just coloured, then drain on absorbent kitchen paper.

Discard all but 2 tablespoons of the oil in the wok. Return to the heat. Add the paste and stir-fry for 5 minutes. Add the duck and stir-fry for 2 minutes. Add the bamboo shoots and stir-fry for 2 minutes. Season to taste with salt and pepper. Turn into a warmed serving dish, garnish with a sprig of fresh coriander and serve immediately with rice.

*Try this:* FOR AN ALTERNATIVE: 268  FOR A LIGHT BITE: 62

# Thai Chicken Fried Rice

**SERVES 4**

175 g/6 oz boneless, chicken breast
2 tbsp vegetable oil
2 garlic cloves, peeled and finely chopped
2 tsp medium curry paste

450 g/1 lb cold cooked rice
1 tbsp light soy sauce
2 tbsp Thai fish sauce
large pinch of sugar
freshly ground black pepper
2 spring onions, trimmed

and shredded lengthways, to garnish
½ small onion, peeled and very finely sliced, to garnish

Using a sharp knife, trim the chicken, discarding any sinew or fat and cut into small cubes. Reserve.

Heat a wok or large frying pan, add the oil and when hot, add the garlic and cook for 10–20 seconds or until just golden. Add the curry paste and stir-fry for a few seconds. Add the chicken and stir-fry for 3–4 minutes, or until tender and the chicken has turned white.

Stir the cold cooked rice into the chicken mixture, then add the soy sauce, fish sauce and sugar, stirring well after each addition. Stir-fry for 2–3 minutes, or until the chicken is cooked through and the rice is piping hot.

Check the seasoning and, if necessary, add a little extra soy sauce. Turn the rice and chicken mixture into a warmed serving dish. Season lightly with black pepper and garnish with shredded spring onion and onion slices. Serve immediately.

*Try this:* FOR AN ALTERNATIVE: 360  FOR A LIGHT BITE: 72

# Chicken in Black Bean Sauce

**SERVES 4**

450 g/1 lb skinless, boneless chicken breast fillets, cut into strips
1 tbsp light soy sauce
2 tbsp Chinese rice wine or dry sherry
salt
1 tsp caster sugar
1 tsp sesame oil
2 tsp cornflour

2 tbsp sunflower oil
2 green peppers, deseeded and diced
1 tbsp freshly grated root ginger
2 garlic cloves, peeled and roughly chopped
2 shallots, peeled and finely chopped
4 spring onions, trimmed

and finely sliced
3 tbsp salted black beans, chopped
150 ml/¼ pint chicken stock
shredded spring onions, to garnish
freshly cooked egg noodles, to serve

Place the chicken strips in a large bowl. Mix together the soy sauce, Chinese rice wine or sherry, a little salt, caster sugar, sesame oil and cornflour and pour over the chicken.

Heat the wok over a high heat, add the oil and when very hot, add the chicken strips and stir-fry for 2 minutes. Add the green peppers and stir-fry for a further 2 minutes. Then add the ginger, garlic, shallots, spring onions and black beans and continue to stir-fry for another 2 minutes.

Add 4 tablespoons of the stock, stir-fry for 1 minute, then pour in the remaining stock and bring to the boil. Reduce the heat and simmer the sauce for 3–4 minutes, or until the chicken is cooked and the sauce has thickened slightly. Garnish with the shredded spring onions and serve immediately with noodles.

*Try this:* FOR AN ALTERNATIVE: 206 FOR A LIGHT BITE: 20

# Green Chicken Curry

**SERVES 4**

1 onion, peeled and chopped
3 lemon grass stalks, outer leaves discarded and finely sliced
2 garlic cloves, peeled and finely chopped
1 tbsp freshly grated

root ginger
3 green chillies
zest and juice of 1 lime
2 tbsp groundnut oil
2 tbsp Thai fish sauce
6 tbsp freshly chopped coriander
6 tbsp freshly chopped basil

450 g/1 lb skinless, boneless chicken breasts, cut into strips
125 g /4 oz fine green beans, trimmed
400 ml can coconut milk
fresh basil leaves, to garnish
freshly cooked rice, to serve

Place the onion, lemon grass, garlic, ginger, chillies, lime zest and juice, 1 tablespoon of groundnut oil, the fish sauce, coriander and basil in a food processor. Blend to a form a smooth paste, which should be of a spoonable consistency. If the sauce looks thick, add a little water. Remove and reserve.

Heat the wok, add the remaining 1 tablespoon of oil and when hot add the chicken. Stir-fry for 2–3 minutes, until the chicken starts to colour, then add the green beans and stir-fry for a further minute. Remove the chicken and beans from the wok and reserve. Wipe the wok clean with absorbent kitchen paper.

Spoon the reserved green paste into the wok and heat for 1 minute. Add the coconut milk and whisk to blend. Return the chicken and beans to the wok and bring to the boil. Simmer for 5–7 minutes, or until the chicken is cooked. Sprinkle with basil leaves and serve immediately with freshly cooked rice.

*Try this:* FOR AN ALTERNATIVE: 232  FOR A LIGHT BITE: 22

# Chicken Chow Mein

**SERVES 4**

225 g/8 oz egg noodles
5 tsp sesame oil
4 tsp light soy sauce
2 tbsp Chinese rice wine or
  dry sherry
salt and freshly ground black
  pepper
225 g/8 oz skinless chicken

breast fillets, cut into
  strips
3 tbsp groundnut oil
2 garlic cloves, peeled and
  finely chopped
50 g/2 oz mangetout peas,
  finely sliced
50 g/2 oz cooked ham, cut

into fine strips
2 tsp dark soy sauce
pinch of sugar

To garnish:
shredded spring onions
toasted sesame seeds

Bring a large saucepan of water to the boil and add the noodles. Cook for 3–5 minutes, drain and plunge into cold water. Drain again, add 1 tablespoon of the sesame oil and stir lightly.

Place 2 teaspoons of light soy sauce, 1 tablespoon of Chinese rice wine or sherry, and 1 teaspoon of the sesame oil, with seasoning to taste in a bowl. Add the chicken and stir well. Cover lightly and leave to marinate in the refrigerator for about 15 minutes.

Heat the wok over a high heat, add 1 tablespoon of the groundnut oil and when very hot, add the chicken and its marinade and stir-fry for 2 minutes. Remove the chicken and juices and reserve. Wipe the wok clean with absorbent kitchen paper.

Reheat the wok and add the oil. Add the garlic and toss in the oil for 20 seconds. Add the mangetout peas and the ham and stir-fry for 1 minute. Add the noodles, remaining light soy sauce, Chinese rice wine or sherry, the dark soy sauce and sugar. Season to taste with salt and pepper and stir-fry for 2 minutes.

Add the chicken and juices to the wok and stir-fry for 4 minutes, or until the chicken is cooked. Drizzle over the remaining sesame oil. Garnish with spring onions and sesame seeds and serve.

*Try this:* FOR AN ALTERNATIVE: 290  FOR A LIGHT BITE: 52

# Chicken Satay Salad

**SERVES 4**

4 tbsp crunchy peanut butter
1 tbsp chilli sauce
1 garlic clove, peeled
   and crushed
2 tbsp cider vinegar
2 tbsp light soy sauce
2 tbsp dark soy sauce

2 tsp soft brown sugar
pinch of salt
2 tsp freshly ground
   Sichuan peppercorns
450 g/1 lb dried egg noodles
2 tbsp sesame oil
1 tbsp groundnut oil

450 g/1 lb skinless, boneless
   chicken breast fillets, cut
   into cubes
shredded celery leaves,
   to garnish
cos lettuce, to serve

Place the peanut butter, chilli sauce, garlic, cider vinegar, soy sauces, sugar, salt and ground peppercorns in a food processor and blend to form a smooth paste. Scrape into a bowl, cover and chill in the refrigerator until required.

Bring a large saucepan of lightly salted water to the boil. Add the noodles and cook for 3–5 minutes. Drain and plunge into cold water. Drain again and toss in the sesame oil. Leave to cool.

Heat the wok until very hot, add the oil and when hot, add the chicken cubes. Stir-fry for 5–6 minutes until the chicken is golden brown and cooked through.

Remove the chicken from the wok using a slotted spoon and add to the noodles, together with the peanut sauce. Mix lightly together, then sprinkle with the shredded celery leaves and either serve immediately or leave until cold, then serve with cos lettuce.

*Try this:* FOR AN ALTERNATIVE: 298  FOR A LIGHT BITE: 32

# Duck in Crispy Wonton Shells

**SERVES 4**

2 x 175 g/6 oz duck breasts
2 tbsp Chinese five
   spice powder
2 tbsp Sichuan peppercorns
1 tsp whole black
   peppercorns

3 tbsp cumin seeds
5 tbsp sea salt
6 slices fresh root ginger
6 spring onions,
   roughly chopped
1 tbsp cornflour

1 litre/1¾ pints vegetable oil
   for frying
16 wonton wrappers
5 cm/2 inch piece cucumber,
   cut into fine strips
125 ml/4 fl oz hoisin sauce

Rinse the duck and dry thoroughly with absorbent kitchen paper. Place the Chinese five spice powder, peppercorns, cumin seeds and salt in a pestle and mortar and crush. Rub the spice mix all over the duck. Wrap in clingfilm and refrigerate for 24 hours.

Place a rack in the wok and pour in boiling water to a depth of 5 cm/2 inches. Place the duck breasts with the ginger slices and 3 chopped spring onions in a heatproof dish on top of the rack. Cover and steam for 40–50 minutes, or until the duck is cooked. Pour off any excess fat from time to time and add more water if necessary. Remove the duck and leave until cooled.

Dust the duck breasts with cornflour, shaking off the excess. Heat the wok, add the oil and, when almost smoking, deep-fry the duck for 8 minutes. Drain, then shred the meat into bite-sized pieces. Shred the remaining spring onions.

Reheat the oil until smoking. Working with 1 wonton at a time, insert 2 wooden skewers into each one, hold in a taco shape and lower into the oil. Hold in the oil until crisp and golden brown. Drain on absorbent kitchen paper. Repeat with the remaining wontons. Fill the wontons with the duck, topped with the spring onions, cucumber and hoisin sauce and serve immediately.

*Try this:* FOR AN ALTERNATIVE: 322   FOR A LIGHT BITE: 24

# Chicken & Baby Vegetable Stir Fry

**SERVES 4**

2 tbsp groundnut oil
1 small red chilli, deseeded
  and finely chopped
150 g/5 oz chicken breast
  or thigh meat, skinned
  and cut into cubes
2 baby leeks, trimmed
  and sliced
12 asparagus spears, halved

125 g/4 oz mangetout
  peas, trimmed
125 g/4 oz baby carrots,
  trimmed and halved
  lengthways
125 g/4 oz fine green
  beans, trimmed and
  diagonally sliced
125 g/4 oz baby sweetcorn,

  diagonally halved
50 ml/2 fl oz chicken stock
2 tsp light soy sauce
1 tbsp dry sherry
1 tsp sesame oil
toasted sesame seeds,
  to garnish

Heat the wok until very hot and add the oil. Add the chopped chilli and chicken and stir-fry for 4–5 minutes, or until the chicken is cooked and golden.

Increase the heat, add the leeks to the chicken and stir-fry for 2 minutes. Add the asparagus spears, mangetout peas, baby carrots, green beans, and baby sweetcorn. Stir-fry for 3–4 minutes, or until the vegetables soften slightly but still retain a slight crispness.

In a small bowl, mix together the chicken stock, soy sauce, dry sherry and sesame oil. Pour into the wok, stir and cook until heated through. Sprinkle with the toasted sesame seeds and serve immediately.

*Try this:* FOR AN ALTERNATIVE: 164 FOR A LIGHT BITE: 52

# Sweet-&-Sour Turkey

**SERVES 4**

2 tbsp groundnut oil
2 garlic cloves, peeled
    and chopped
1 tbsp freshly grated
    root ginger
4 spring onions, trimmed
    and cut into 4 cm/1½
    inch lengths

450 g/1 lb turkey breast,
    skinned and cut into strips
1 red pepper, deseeded
    and cut into 2.5 cm/1
    inch squares
225 g/8 oz canned water
    chestnuts, drained
150 ml/¼ pint chicken stock

2 tbsp Chinese rice wine
3 tbsp light soy sauce
2 tsp dark soy sauce
2 tbsp tomato paste
2 tbsp white wine vinegar
1 tbsp sugar
1 tbsp cornflour
egg-fried rice, to serve

Heat the wok over a high heat, add the oil and when hot, add the garlic, ginger and spring onions, stir-fry for 20 seconds.

Add the turkey to the wok and stir-fry for 2 minutes, or until beginning to colour. Add the peppers and water chestnuts and stir-fry for a further 2 minutes.

Mix the chicken stock, Chinese rice wine, light and dark soy sauce, tomato paste, white wine vinegar and the sugar together in a small jug or bowl. Add the mixture to the wok, stir and bring the sauce to the boil.

Mix together the cornflour with 2 tablespoons of water and add to the wok. Reduce the heat and simmer for 3 minutes, or until the turkey is cooked thoroughly and the sauce slightly thickened and glossy. Serve immediately with egg-fried rice.

*Try this:* FOR AN ALTERNATIVE: 378  FOR A LIGHT BITE: 78

# Thai Coconut Chicken

**SERVES 4**

1 tsp cumin seeds
1 tsp mustard seeds
1 tsp coriander seeds
1 tsp turmeric
1 bird's-eye chilli, deseeded
   and finely chopped
1 tbsp freshly grated
   root ginger

2 garlic cloves, peeled and
   finely chopped
125 ml/4 fl oz double cream
8 skinless chicken thighs
2 tbsp groundnut oil
1 onion, peeled and
   finely sliced
200 ml/7 fl oz coconut milk

salt and freshly ground
   black pepper
4 tbsp freshly chopped
   coriander
2 spring onions, shredded,
   to garnish
freshly cooked Thai fragrant
   rice, to serve

Heat the wok and add the cumin seeds, mustard seeds and coriander seeds. Dry-fry over a low to medium heat for 2 minutes, or until the fragrance becomes stronger and the seeds start to pop. Add the turmeric and leave to cool slightly. Grind the spices in a pestle and mortar or blend to a fine powder in a food processor.

Mix the chilli, ginger, garlic and the cream together in a small bowl, add the ground spices and mix. Place the chicken thighs in a shallow dish and spread the spice paste over the thighs.

Heat the wok over a high heat, add the oil and when hot, add the onion and stir-fry until golden brown. Add the chicken and spice paste. Cook for 5–6 minutes, stirring occasionally, until evenly coloured. Add the coconut milk and season to taste with salt and pepper. Simmer the chicken for 15–20 minutes, or until the thighs are cooked through, taking care not to allow the mixture to boil. Stir in the chopped coriander and serve immediately with the freshly cooked rice sprinkled with shredded spring onions.

*Try this:* FOR AN ALTERNATIVE: 246   FOR A LIGHT BITE: 58

# Noodles with Turkey & Mushrooms

**SERVES 4**

225 g/8 oz dried egg noodles
1 tbsp groundnut oil
1 red onion, peeled
   and sliced
2 tbsp freshly grated
   root ginger
3 garlic cloves, peeled and

finely chopped
350 g/12 oz turkey breast,
   skinned and cut into strips
125 g/4 oz baby button
   mushrooms
150 g/5 oz chestnut
   mushrooms

2 tbsp dark soy sauce
2 tbsp hoisin sauce
2 tbsp dry sherry
4 tbsp vegetable stock
2 tsp cornflour

Bring a large saucepan of lightly salted water to the boil and add the noodles. Cook for 3–5 minutes, then drain and plunge immediately into cold water. When cool, drain again and reserve.

Heat the wok, add the oil and when hot, add the onion and stir-fry for 3 minutes until it starts to soften. Add the ginger and garlic and stir-fry for a further 3 minutes, then add the turkey strips and stir-fry for 4–5 minutes until sealed and golden.

Wipe and slice the chestnut mushrooms into similar-sized pieces and add to the wok with the whole button mushrooms. Stir-fry for 3–4 minutes, or until tender. When all the vegetables are tender and the turkey is cooked, add the soy sauce, hoisin sauce, sherry and vegetable stock.

Mix the cornflour with 2 tablespoons of water and add to the wok, then cook, stirring, until the sauce thickens. Add the drained noodles to the wok, then toss the mixture together and serve immediately.

*Try this:* FOR AN ALTERNATIVE: 348  FOR A LIGHT BITE: 64

# Chicken & Cashew Nuts

**SERVES 4**

450 g/1 lb skinless chicken, boneless breast fillets, cut into 1 cm/½ inch cubes
1 medium egg white, beaten
1 tsp salt
1 tsp sesame oil
2 tsp cornflour

300 ml/½ pint groundnut oil for deep frying
2 tsp sunflower oil
50 g/2 oz unsalted cashews
4 spring onions, shredded
50 g/2 oz mangetout peas, diagonally sliced

1 tbsp Chinese rice wine
1 tbsp light soy sauce
shredded spring onions, to garnish
freshly steamed white rice with fresh coriander leaves, to serve

Place the cubes of chicken in a large bowl. Add the egg white, salt, sesame oil and cornflour. Mix well to ensure the chicken is coated thoroughly. Chill in the refrigerator for 20 minutes.

Heat the wok until very hot, add the groundnut oil and when hot, remove the wok from the heat and add the chicken. Stir continuously to prevent the chicken from sticking to the wok. When the chicken turns white, after about 2 minutes, remove it using a slotted spoon and reserve. Discard the oil.

Wipe the wok clean with absorbent kitchen paper and heat it again until very hot. Add the sunflower oil and heat. When hot, add the cashew nuts, spring onions and mangetout peas and stir-fry for 1 minute.

Add the rice wine and soy sauce. Return the chicken to the wok and stir-fry for 2 minutes. Garnish with shredded spring onions and serve immediately with freshly steamed rice sprinkled with fresh coriander.

*Try this:* FOR AN ALTERNATIVE: 212  FOR A LIGHT BITE: 22

# Szechuan Turkey Noodles

**SERVES 4**

1 tbsp tomato paste
2 tsp black bean sauce
2 tsp cider vinegar
salt and freshly ground
    black pepper
½ tsp Szechuan pepper
2 tsp sugar
4 tsp sesame oil

225 g/8 oz dried egg noodles
2 tbsp groundnut oil
2 tsp freshly grated
    root ginger
3 garlic cloves, peeled and
    roughly chopped
2 shallots, peeled and
    finely chopped

2 courgettes, trimmed and
    cut into fine matchsticks
450 g/1 lb turkey breast,
    skinned and cut into strips
deep-fried onion rings,
    to garnish

Mix together the tomato paste, black bean sauce, cider vinegar, a pinch of salt and pepper, the sugar and half the sesame oil. Chill in the refrigerator for 30 minutes.

Bring a large saucepan of lightly salted water to the boil and add the noodles. Cook for 3–5 minutes, drain and plunge immediately into cold water. Toss with the remaining sesame oil and reserve.

Heat the wok until very hot, then add the oil and when hot, add the ginger, garlic and shallots. Stir-fry for 20 seconds, then add the courgettes and turkey strips. Stir-fry for 3–4 minutes, or until the turkey strips are sealed.

Add the prepared chilled black bean sauce and continue to stir-fry for another 4 minutes over a high heat. Add the drained noodles to the wok and stir until the noodles, turkey, vegetables and the sauce are well mixed together. Garnish with the deep-fried onion rings and serve immediately.

*Try this:* FOR AN ALTERNATIVE: 260  FOR A LIGHT BITE: 66

# Lime & Sesame Turkey

**SERVES 4**

450 g/1 lb turkey breast, skinned and cut into strips
2 lemon grass stalks, outer leaves discarded and finely sliced
grated zest of 1 lime
4 garlic cloves, peeled and crushed

6 shallots, peeled and finely sliced
2 tbsp Thai fish sauce
2 tsp soft brown sugar
1 small red chilli, deseeded and finely sliced
3 tbsp sunflower oil
1 tbsp sesame oil

225 g/8 oz stir-fry rice noodles
1 tbsp sesame seeds
shredded spring onions, t o garnish
freshly stir-fried vegetables, to serve

Place the turkey strips in a shallow dish. Mix together the lemon grass stalks, lime zest, garlic, shallots, Thai fish sauce, sugar and chilli with 2 tablespoons of the sunflower oil and the sesame oil. Pour over the turkey. Cover and leave to marinate in the refrigerator for 2–3 hours, spooning the marinade over the turkey occasionally.

Soak the noodles in warm water for 5 minutes. Drain through a sieve or colander, then plunge immediately into cold water. Drain again and reserve until ready to use.

Heat the wok until very hot and add the sesame seeds. Dry-fry for 1–2 minutes, or until toasted in colour. Remove from the wok and reserve. Wipe the wok to remove any dust left from the seeds.

Heat the wok again and add the remaining sunflower oil. When hot, drain the turkey from the marinade and stir-fry for 3–4 minutes, or until golden brown and cooked through (you may need to do this in 2 batches). When all the turkey has been cooked, add the noodles to the wok and cook, stirring, for 1–2 minutes, or until heated through thoroughly. Garnish with the shredded spring onions, toasted sesame seeds and serve immediately with freshly stir-fried vegetables of your choice.

*Try this:* FOR AN ALTERNATIVE: 274 FOR A LIGHT BITE: 68

# Hoisin Duck & Greens Stir Fry

**SERVES 4**

350 g/12 oz duck breasts,
 skinned and cut into strips
1 medium egg white, beaten
½ tsp salt
1 tsp sesame oil
2 tsp cornflour
2 tbsp groundnut oil

2 tbsp freshly grated
 root ginger
50 g/2 oz bamboo shoots
50 g/2 oz fine green
 beans, trimmed
50 g/2 oz pak choi, trimmed
2 tbsp hoisin sauce

1 tsp Chinese rice wine or
 dry sherry
zest and juice of ½ orange
strips of orange zest,
 to garnish
freshly steamed egg
 noodles, to serve

Place the duck strips in a shallow dish, then add the egg white, salt, sesame oil and cornflour. Stir lightly until the duck is coated in the mixture. Cover and chill in the refrigerator for 20 minutes.

Heat the wok until very hot and add the oil. Remove the wok from the heat and add the duck, stirring continuously to prevent the duck from sticking to the wok. Add the ginger and stir-fry for 2 minutes. Add the bamboo shoots, the green beans and the pak choi, and stir-fry for 1–2 minutes until wilted.

Mix together the hoisin sauce, the Chinese rice wine or sherry and the orange zest and juice. Pour into the wok and stir to coat the duck and vegetables. Stir-fry for 1–2 minutes, or until the duck and vegetables are tender. Garnish with the strips of orange zest and serve immediately with freshly steamed egg noodles.

*Try this:* FOR AN ALTERNATIVE: 362  FOR A LIGHT BITE: 80

# Duck & Exotic Fruit Stir Fry

**SERVES 4**

4 duck breast fillets, skinned
    removed and cut
    into strips
½ tsp Chinese five
    spice powder
2 tbsp soy sauce
1 tbsp sesame oil
1 tbsp groundnut oil

2 celery stalks, trimmed
    and diced
225 g can pineapples
    chunks, drained
1 mango, peeled, stoned
    and cut into chunks
125 g/4 oz lychees, peeled if
    fresh, stoned and halved

125 ml/4 fl oz chicken stock
2 tbsp tomato paste
2 tbsp plum sauce
2 tsp wine vinegar
pinch of soft brown sugar
toasted nuts, to garnish
steamed rice, to serve

Place the duck strips in a shallow bowl. Mix together the Chinese five spice powder, soy sauce and sesame oil, pour over the duck and marinate for 2 hours in the refrigerator. Stir occasionally during marinating. Remove the duck from the marinade and reserve.

Heat the wok, add the oil and when hot, stir-fry the marinated duck strips for 4 minutes. Remove from the wok and reserve.

Add the celery to the wok and stir-fry for 2 minutes, then add the pineapple, mango and lychees and stir-fry for a further 3 minutes. Return the duck to the wok.

Mix together the chicken stock, tomato paste, plum sauce, wine vinegar and a pinch of brown sugar. Add to the wok, bring to the boil and simmer, stirring, for 2 minutes. Sprinkle with the nuts and serve immediately with the freshly steamed rice.

*Try this:* FOR AN ALTERNATIVE: 372   FOR A LIGHT BITE: 80

# Teriyaki Duck with Plum Chutney

**SERVES 4**

4 tbsp Japanese soy sauce
4 tbsp dry sherry
2 garlic cloves, peeled and finely chopped
2.5 cm/1 inch piece fresh root ginger, peeled and finely chopped
350 g/12 oz skinless duck breast fillets, cut in chunks

2 tbsp groundnut oil
225 g/8 oz carrots, peeled and cut into fine strips
½ cucumber, cut into strips
5 spring onions, trimmed and shredded
toasted almonds, to garnish
freshly cooked egg noodles, to serve

**For the plum chutney:**
25 g/1 oz butter
1 red onion, peeled and finely chopped
2 tsp soft brown sugar
4 plums, stoned and halved
zest and juice of ½ orange
50 g/2 oz raisins

Mix together the soy sauce, sherry, garlic and ginger and pour into a shallow dish. Add the duck strips and stir until coated in the marinade. Cover and leave in the refrigerator for 30 minutes.

Meanwhile make the plum chutney. Melt the butter in a wok, add the onion and sugar and cook gently over a low heat for 20 minutes. Add the plums, orange zest and juice and simmer for 10 minutes, then stir in the raisins. Spoon into a small bowl and wipe the wok clean. Drain the duck, reserving the marinade.

Heat the wok, add the oil and when hot, add the carrots, cucumber and spring onions. Stir-fry for 2 minutes, or until tender. Remove and reserve.

Add the drained duck to the wok and stir-fry over a high heat for 2 minutes. Return the vegetables to the wok and add the reserved marinade. Stir-fry briefly, until heated through.

Garnish the duck with the toasted almonds and serve immediately with freshly cooked noodles and the plum chutney.

*Try this:* FOR AN ALTERNATIVE: 228   FOR A LIGHT BITE: 80

# Steamed, Crispy, Citrus Chicken

**SERVES 6**

200 ml/7 fl oz light soy sauce
1 tbsp brown sugar
4 star anise
2 slices fresh root
    ginger, peeled
5 spring onions, trimmed
    and sliced

1 small orange, cut
    into wedges
1 lime, cut into wedges
1.1 kg/2½ lb chicken
2 garlic cloves, peeled and
    finely chopped
2 tbsp Chinese rice wine

2 tbsp dark soy sauce
300 ml/½ pint groundnut oil
orange slices, to garnish
freshly cooked steamed rice,
    to serve

Pour the light soy sauce and 200 ml/7 fl oz water into the wok and add the sugar and star anise. Bring to the boil over a gentle heat. Pour into a small bowl and leave to cool slightly. Wipe the wok clean with absorbent kitchen paper.

Put the ginger, 2 spring onions, orange and lime inside the cavity of the chicken. Place a rack in the wok and pour in boiling water to a depth of 5 cm/2 inches. Put a piece of tinfoil onto the rack and place the chicken in the centre, then pour over the soy sauce mixture.

Cover the wok and steam gently for 1–1 hour 10 minutes, or until the chicken is cooked through, pouring off excess fat from time to time. Add more water if necessary. Leave the chicken to cool and dry for up to 3 hours, then cut the chicken into quarters.

Mix together the garlic, Chinese rice wine, dark soy sauce and remaining spring onions, then reserve. Dry the wok and heat again, then add the oil. When hot, shallow fry the chicken quarters for 4 minutes, or until golden and crisp. Do this 1 portion at a time, remove and drain on absorbent kitchen paper.

When cool enough to handle shred into bite-sized pieces and drizzle over the sauce. Garnish with slices of orange and serve with freshly steamed rice.

*Try this:* FOR AN ALTERNATIVE: 214  FOR A LIGHT BITE: 50

# Rice & Noodles

# Thai Spring Rolls with Noodles & Dipping Sauce

**MAKES ABOUT 30**

50 g/2 oz dried rice vermicelli
1 carrot, peeled and cut into matchsticks
50 g/2 oz mangetout peas, thinly shredded lengthways
3 spring onions, trimmed and finely chopped

125 g/4 oz peeled prawns, thawed if frozen
2 garlic cloves, peeled and crushed
1 tsp sesame oil
2 tbsp light soy sauce
1 tsp chilli sauce
200 g/7 oz filo pastry, cut

into 15 cm/6 inch squares
1 medium egg white, lightly beaten
vegetable oil for deep frying
sprigs of fresh coriander, to garnish
sweet chilli sauce, for dipping

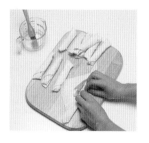

Cook the rice vermicelli according to the packet directions, then drain thoroughly. Roughly chop and reserve. Bring a saucepan of lightly salted water to the boil and blanch the carrot and mangetout peas for 1 minute. Drain and refresh under cold water, then drain again and pat dry on absorbent kitchen paper. Mix together with the noodles. Add the spring onions, prawns, garlic, sesame oil, soy sauce and chilli sauce and reserve.

Fold the filo pastry squares in half diagonally to form triangles. Lay a triangle with the fold facing you and place a spoonful of the mixture in the centre. Roll over the long end of the wrapper to enclose the filling, then bring over the corners to enclose the ends of the roll. Brush the point of the spring roll furthest from you with a little beaten egg white and continue rolling to seal.

Fill a wok about a third full with vegetable oil and heat to 190°C/375°F, or until a cube of bread browns in 30 seconds. Fry the spring rolls, 4 or 5 at a time, for 1–2 minutes, or until golden and crisp. Drain on absorbent kitchen paper. Fry the remaining spring rolls in batches. Garnish with sprigs of coriander and serve hot with the dark soy sauce and sweet chilli sauce.

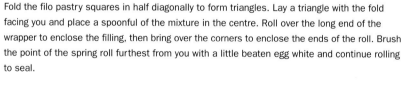

*Try this:* FOR AN ALTERNATIVE: 96  FOR A LIGHT BITE: 56

# Singapore Noodles

**SERVES 4**

225 g/8 oz flat rice noodles
3 tbsp sunflower oil
2 shallots, peeled and sliced
2 garlic cloves, peeled
    and crushed
2 tbsp freshly grated
    root ginger
1 red pepper, deseeded and

finely sliced
1 hot red chilli, deseeded
    and finely chopped
175 g/6 oz peeled
    raw prawns
125 g/4 oz boneless
    pork, diced
175 g/6 oz boneless

chicken, diced
1 tbsp curry powder
1 tsp each crushed fennel
    seeds and ground
    cinnamon
50 g/2 oz frozen peas, thawed
juice of 1 lemon
3 tbsp fresh coriander leaves

Put the noodles into a large bowl and pour over boiling water to cover. Leave to stand for 3 minutes, or until slightly underdone according to the packet directions. Drain well and reserve.

Heat a wok until almost smoking. Add the oil and carefully swirl around to coat the sides of the wok. Add the shallots, garlic and ginger and cook for a few seconds. Add the pepper and chilli and stir-fry for 3–4 minutes, or until the pepper has softened.

Add the prawns, pork, chicken and curry powder to the wok. Stir-fry for a further 4–5 minutes until the meat and prawns are coloured on all sides. Then add the fennel seeds and the ground cinnamon and stir to mix.

Add the drained noodles to the wok along with the peas and cook for a further 1–2 minutes until heated through. Add the lemon juice to taste. Sprinkle with the fresh coriander leaves and serve immediately.

*Try this:* FOR AN ALTERNATIVE: 302  FOR A LIGHT BITE: 66

# Oriental Noodle & Peanut Salad with Coriander

**SERVES 4**

350 g/12 oz rice vermicelli
1 litre/1¾ pints light
   chicken stock
2 tsp sesame oil
2 tbsp light soy sauce
8 spring onions

3 tbsp groundnut oil
2 hot green chillis, deseeded
   and thinly sliced
25 g/1 oz roughly
   chopped coriander
2 tbsp freshly chopped mint

125 g/4 oz cucumber,
   finely chopped
40 g/1½ oz beansprouts
40 g/1½ oz roasted peanuts,
   roughly chopped

Put the noodles into a large bowl. Bring the stock to the boil and immediately pour over the noodles. Leave to soak for 4 minutes, or according to the packet directions. Drain well, discarding the stock or saving it for another use. Mix together the sesame oil and soy sauce and pour over the hot noodles. Toss well to coat and leave until cold.

Trim and thinly slice 4 of the spring onions. Heat the oil in a wok over a low heat. Add the spring onions and, as soon as they sizzle, remove from the heat and leave to cool. When cold, toss with the noodles.

On a chopping board, cut the remaining spring onions lengthways 4–6 times, leave in a bowl of cold water until tassels form. Serve the noodles in individual bowls, each dressed with a little chilli, coriander, mint, cucumber, beansprouts and peanuts. Garnish with the spring onion tassels and serve.

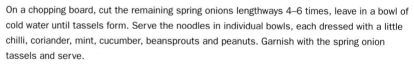

*Try this:* FOR AN ALTERNATIVE: 308  FOR A LIGHT BITE: 52

# Char Sui Pork & Noodle Salad

**SERVES 4**

200 g/7 oz flat rice noodles
4 tbsp black treacle
2 tbsp dark soy sauce
3 tbsp Chinese rice wine or
   dry sherry
3 star anise, roughly crushed
1 cinnamon stick
350 g/12 oz pork tenderloin,

in 1 piece
1 tbsp groundnut oil
2 garlic cloves, peeled and
   finely chopped
1 tsp freshly grated
   root ginger
3 spring onions, trimmed
   and sliced

125 g/4 oz pak choi,
   roughly chopped
2 tbsp light soy sauce
fresh coriander leaves,
   to garnish
prepared or bought plum
   sauce (see page 272),
   to serve

Preheat the oven to 220°C/425°F/Gas Mark 7, 15 minutes before cooking. Soak the noodles in boiling water according to the packet directions. Drain and reserve. Place the treacle, soy sauce, Chinese rice wine or sherry, star anise and cinnamon into a small saucepan and stir over a gentle heat until mixed thoroughly, then reserve. Trim the pork tenderloin of any excess fat and put into a shallow dish. Pour the cooled sauce over the tenderloin. Turn the pork, making sure it is completely coated in the sauce. Place in the refrigerator and leave to marinate for 4 hours, turning occasionally.

Remove the pork from its marinade and transfer to a roasting tin. Roast in the preheated oven for 12–14 minutes, basting once, until the pork is cooked through. Remove from the oven and leave until just warm.

Heat the wok, add the oil and when hot, add the garlic, ginger and spring onions. Stir-fry for 30 seconds before adding the pak choi. Stir-fry for a further 1 minute until the pak choi has wilted, then add the noodles and soy sauce. Toss for a few seconds until well mixed, then transfer to a large serving dish. Leave to cool.

Thickly slice the pork fillet and add to the cooled noodles. Garnish with coriander leaves and serve with plum sauce.

*Try this:* FOR AN ALTERNATIVE: 144  FOR A LIGHT BITE: 66

# Thai Rice Cakes with Mango Salsa

**SERVES 4**

225 g/8 oz Thai fragrant rice
400 g can coconut milk
1 lemon grass stalk, bruised
2 kaffir lime leaves, shredded
1 tbsp vegetable oil, plus extra for deep frying
1 garlic clove, peeled and finely chopped

1 tsp freshly grated root ginger
1 red pepper, deseeded and finely chopped
2 red chillies, deseeded and finely chopped
1 medium egg, beaten
25 g/1 oz dried breadcrumbs

**For the mango salsa:**
1 large mango, peeled, stoned and finely chopped
1 small red onion, peeled and finely chopped
2 tbsp freshly chopped coriander
2 tbsp freshly chopped basil
juice of 1 lime

Wash the rice in several changes of water until the water stays relatively clear. Drain, place in a saucepan with a tight-fitting lid and add the coconut milk, lemon grass and lime leaves. Bring to the boil, cover and cook over the lowest possible heat for 10 minutes. Turn off the heat and leave to stand for 10 minutes, without lifting the lid.

Heat the wok, then add 1 tablespoon of oil and when hot, add the garlic, ginger, red pepper and half the chilli. Stir-fry for 1–2 minutes until just softened then place in a large bowl.

When the rice is cooked, turn into the mixing bowl and add the egg. Season to taste with salt and pepper and mix together well. Put the breadcrumbs into a shallow dish. Form the rice mixture into 8 cakes and coat them in the breadcrumbs. Chill the cakes in the refrigerator for 30 minutes.

Meanwhile, make the mango salsa. In a bowl, mix together the mango, red onion, coriander, basil, lime juice and remaining red chilli and reserve.

Fill a clean wok about one-third full of vegetable oil. Heat to 190°C/375°F, or until a cube of bread browns in 30 seconds. Cook the rice cakes, 1 or 2 at a time, for 2–3 minutes until golden and crisp. Drain on absorbent kitchen paper. Serve with the mango salsa.

*Try this:* FOR AN ALTERNATIVE: 324   FOR A LIGHT BITE: 36

# Thai Fried Rice
# with Prawns & Chillies

**SERVES 4**

350 g/12 oz Thai fragrant rice
2 tbsp groundnut or
    vegetable oil
2 garlic cloves, peeled and
    finely chopped
2 red chillies, deseeded and
    finely chopped

125 g/4 oz peeled
    raw prawns
1 tbsp Thai fish sauce
¼ tsp sugar
1 tbsp light soy sauce
½ small onion, peeled and
    finely sliced

½ red pepper, deseeded and
    finely sliced
1 spring onion, green part
    only, cut into long strips
sprigs of fresh coriander,
    to garnish

Wash the rice in several changes of water until the water remains relatively clear. Drain well. Bring a large saucepan of salted water to the boil and add the rice. Cook for 12–15 minutes until tender. Drain well and reserve.

Heat a wok, add the oil and when very hot, add the garlic and stir-fry for 20 seconds, or until just browned. Add the chillies and prawns and stir-fry for 2–3 minutes.

Add the fish sauce, sugar and soy sauce and stir-fry for another 30 seconds, or until the prawns are cooked through.

Add the cooked rice to the wok and stir together well. Then add the onion, red pepper and spring onion, mix together for a further 1 minute, then turn onto a serving platter. Garnish with sprigs of fresh coriander and serve immediately.

*Try this:* FOR AN ALTERNATIVE: 376   FOR A LIGHT BITE: 54

# Chicken with Noodles

**SERVES 2–3**

225 g/8 oz medium
  egg noodles
125 g/4 oz skinless, boneless
  chicken breast fillets
1 tbsp light soy sauce
2 tsp Chinese rice wine or

dry sherry
5 tsp groundnut oil
2 garlic cloves, peeled and
  finely chopped
50 g/2 oz mangetout peas
25 g/1 oz smoked back

bacon, cut into fine strips
½ tsp sugar
2 spring onions, peeled and
  finely chopped
1 tsp sesame oil

Cook the noodles according to the packet directions. Drain and refresh under cold water. Drain again and reserve.

Slice the chicken into fine shreds and mix with 2 teaspoons of the light soy sauce and Chinese rice wine. Leave to marinate in the refrigerator for 10 minutes.

Heat a wok, add 2 teaspoons of the oil and when hot, stir-fry the chicken shreds for about 2 minutes, then transfer to a plate. Wipe the wok clean with absorbent kitchen paper.

Return the wok to the heat and add the remaining oil. Add the garlic, then after 10 seconds add the mangetout peas and bacon. Stir-fry for a further 1 minute, then add the drained noodles, remaining soy sauce, sugar and spring onions. Stir-fry for a further 2 minutes then add the reserved chicken.

Stir-fry for a further 3–4 minutes until the chicken is cooked through. Add the sesame oil and mix together. Serve either hot or cold.

*Try this:* FOR AN ALTERNATIVE: 248   FOR A LIGHT BITE: 20

# Chinese Bean Sauce Noodles

**SERVES 4**

250 g/9oz fine egg noodles
1½ tbsp sesame oil
1 tbsp groundnut oil
3 garlic cloves, peeled and
  finely chopped
4 spring onions, trimmed

and finely chopped
450 g/1 lb fresh pork mince
100 ml/4 fl oz crushed yellow
  bean sauce
1-2 tsp hot chilli sauce
1 tbsp Chinese rice wine or

dry sherry
2 tbsp dark soy sauce
½ tsp cayenne pepper
2 tsp sugar
150 ml/¼ pint chicken stock

Put the noodles into a large bowl and pour over boiling water to cover. Leave to soak according to packet directions until tender. Drain well and place in a bowl with the sesame oil. Toss together well and reserve.

Heat a wok until it is hot, add the groundnut oil and when it is hot, add the garlic and half the spring onions. Stir-fry for a few seconds, then add the pork. Stir well to break up and continue to stir-fry for 1–2 minutes until it changes colour.

Add the yellow bean sauce, chilli sauce, Chinese rice wine or sherry, soy sauce, cayenne pepper, sugar and chicken stock, stirring all the time. Bring to the boil, reduce the heat and simmer for 5 minutes.

Meanwhile, bring a large saucepan of water to the boil and add the noodles for about 20 seconds. Drain well and tip into a warmed serving bowl. Pour the sauce over the top, sprinkle with the remaining spring onions and mix well. Serve immediately.

*Try this:* FOR AN ALTERNATIVE: 248   FOR A LIGHT BITE: 66

# Beef Noodle Soup

**SERVES 4**

900 g/2 lb boneless shin or braising steak
1 cinnamon stick
2 star anise
2 tbsp light soy sauce
6 dried red chillies or

3 fresh, chopped in half
2 dried citrus peels, soaked and diced (optional)
1.1 litre/2 pints beef or chicken stock
350 g/12 oz egg noodles

2 spring onions, trimmed and chopped, to garnish
warm chunks of crusty farmhouse bread, to serve (optional)

Trim the meat of any fat and sinew, then cut into thin strips. Place the meat, cinnamon, star anise, soy sauce, red chillies, chopped citrus peels (if using), and stock into the wok. Bring to the boil, then reduce the heat to a simmer. Skim any fat or scum that floats to the surface. Cover the wok and simmer for about 1½ hours or until the meat is tender.

Meanwhile, bring a saucepan of lightly salted water to the boil, then add the noodles and cook in the boiling water for 3–4 minutes until tender or according to packet directions. Drain well and reserve.

When the meat is tender, add the noodles to the wok and simmer for a further 1–2 minutes until the noodles are heated through thoroughly. Ladle the soup into warm shallow soup bowls or dishes and scatter with chopped spring onions. Serve, if liked, with chunks of warm crusty bread.

*Try this:* FOR AN ALTERNATIVE: 296  FOR A LIGHT BITE: 24

# Chicken Noodle Soup

**SERVES 4**

carcass of a medium-sized cooked chicken
1 large carrot, peeled and roughly chopped
1 medium onion, peeled and quartered
1 leek, trimmed and roughly chopped
2–3 bay leaves
a few black peppercorns
2 litres/3½ pints water
225 g/8 oz Chinese cabbage, trimmed
50 g/2 oz chestnut mushrooms, wiped and sliced
125 g/4 oz cooked chicken, sliced or chopped
50 g/2 oz medium or fine egg thread noodles

Break the chicken carcass into smaller pieces and place in the wok with the carrot, onion, leek, bay leaves, peppercorns and water. Bring slowly to the boil. Skim away any fat or scum that rises for the first 15 minutes. Simmer very gently for 1–1½ hours. If the liquid reduces by more than one third, add a little more water.

Remove from the heat and leave until cold. Strain into a large bowl and chill in the refrigerator until any fat in the stock rises and sets on the surface. Remove the fat and discard. Draw a sheet of absorbent kitchen paper across the surface of the stock to absorb any remaining fat.

Return the stock to the wok and bring to a simmer. Add the Chinese cabbage, mushrooms and chicken and simmer gently for 7–8 minutes until the vegetables are tender.

Meanwhile, cook the noodles according to the packet directions until tender. Drain well. Transfer a portion of noodles to each serving bowl before pouring in some soup and vegetables. Serve immediately.

*Try this:* FOR AN ALTERNATIVE: 294  FOR A LIGHT BITE: 20

# Crispy Noodle Salad

**SERVES 4**

2 tbsp sunflower seeds
2 tbsp pumpkin seeds
50 g/2 oz rice vermicelli or
   stir-fry noodles
175 g/6 oz unsalted butter
2 tbsp sesame seeds,
   lightly toasted

125 g/4 oz red cabbage,
   trimmed and shredded
1 orange pepper, deseeded
   and finely chopped
125 g/4 oz button
   mushrooms, wiped
   and quartered

2 spring onions, trimmed
   and finely chopped
salt and freshly ground
   black pepper
shredded pickled sushi
   ginger, to garnish

Preheat the oven to 200°C/400°F/Gas Mark 6, then sprinkle the sunflower and pumpkin seeds on a baking sheet. Toast in the oven, stirring occasionally, for 10–15 minutes or until lightly toasted. Remove from the oven and leave to cool.

Crush the rice vermicelli into small pieces (this is easiest in a plastic bag or while the noodles are still in the packet), and reserve. Melt the butter in a small saucepan and leave to cool for a few minutes. Pour the clear yellow liquid carefully into a bowl, leaving behind the white milky solids. Discard the milky solids.

Heat the yellow, clarified butter in a wok and fry the crushed noodles in batches until browned, stirring constantly and gently. Remove the fried noodles as they cook, using a slotted spoon, and drain on absorbent kitchen paper. Transfer the noodles to a bowl and add the toasted seeds.

Mix together the red cabbage, orange pepper, button mushrooms and spring onions in a large bowl and season to taste with salt and pepper. Just before serving, add the noodles and seeds to the salad and mix gently. Garnish with a little sushi ginger and serve.

*Try this:* FOR AN ALTERNATIVE: 312 FOR A LIGHT BITE: 66

# Thai Spicy Prawn & Lettuce Noodle Soup

**SERVES 4**

225 g/8 oz raw tiger prawns
1 tbsp groundnut or
   vegetable oil
2 garlic cloves, peeled
   and crushed
1 red chilli, deseeded and
   finely chopped
1 tbsp freshly grated

root ginger
4 spring onions, trimmed
   and finely sliced
1.1 litre/2 pints chicken stock
1 kaffir lime leaf,
   finely shredded
1 lemon grass stalk, outer
   leaves discarded and

finely chopped
75 g/3 oz shiitake
   mushrooms, sliced
125 g/4 oz medium egg
   thread noodles
50 g/2 oz lettuce, shredded
75 g/3 oz beansprouts

Peel the prawns, leaving the tail tip on. Cut almost in half down the back of the prawn, discarding any dark veins and open out. Rinse lightly, then pat dry with absorbent kitchen paper and reserve.

Heat a wok until very hot, then add the oil and when hot, add the garlic, chilli, ginger and spring onions and stir-fry for 30 seconds. Add the prawns and stir-fry for a further 1 minute.

Add the chicken stock, lime leaf and lemon grass and bring to the boil. Reduce the heat and simmer for 10 minutes, adding the mushrooms after 7–8 minutes.

Meanwhile, cook the noodles in plenty of boiling water according to the packet directions. Drain well. Add to the soup with the lettuce and beansprouts and return to the boil; simmer for about 30 seconds. Divide the soup between individual bowls and serve immediately.

*Try this:* FOR AN ALTERNATIVE: 296  FOR A LIGHT BITE: 58

# Seafood Noodle Salad

**SERVES 4**

8 baby squid, cleaned
2 tbsp mirin
2 tbsp rice vinegar
4 tbsp sunflower oil
1 red chilli, deseeded and
    finely chopped
2 garlic cloves, peeled
    and crushed

6 spring onions, trimmed
    and finely sliced
1 red pepper, deseeded and
    finely sliced
1 tbsp turmeric
2 tsp ground coriander
8 raw tiger prawns, peeled
175 g/6 oz medium

    egg noodles
175 g/6 oz fresh white
    crabmeat
50 g/2 oz beansprouts
salt and freshly ground
    black pepper

Remove the tentacles from the squid and reserve. Slit the squid bodies open down one side and open out flat.

Using a small sharp knife, score the flesh diagonally, first in one direction then the other, to make diamond shapes. Place in a bowl with the squid tentacles, mirin, rice vinegar, half the oil and the chilli and leave to marinate in the refrigerator for 1 hour.

Heat a wok until very hot. Add the remaining oil and, when hot, add the garlic, half the spring onions and the red pepper. Stir-fry for 1 minute, then add the turmeric and coriander. Cook for a further 30 seconds before adding the cleaned squid and its marinade and the prawns. Bring to the boil and simmer for 2–3 minutes, or until the squid and prawns are tender. Remove from the heat and leave to cool.

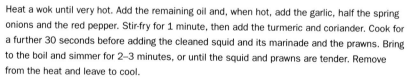

Cook the noodles for 3–4 minutes until tender, or according to packet directions. Drain well and put in a large serving bowl along with the white crabmeat and the cooled squid and prawn mixture. Stir together and leave until cold. Just before serving, add the beansprouts and remaining spring onions with seasoning to taste and serve.

*Try this:* FOR AN ALTERNATIVE: 280 FOR A LIGHT BITE: 24

# Chinese Fried Rice

**SERVES 4**

450 g/1 lb long-grain rice
2 tbsp groundnut oil
50 g/2 oz smoked bacon,
  chopped
2 garlic cloves, peeled and
  finely chopped
1 tsp freshly grated

root ginger
125 g/4 oz frozen peas,
  thawed
2 medium eggs, beaten
125 g/4 oz beansprouts
salt and freshly ground
  black pepper

50 g/2 oz roasted peanuts,
  chopped, to garnish
3 spring onions, trimmed
  and finely chopped,
  to garnish

Wash the rice in several changes of water until it runs relatively clear. Drain well. Put into a saucepan or flameproof casserole dish with a tight-fitting lid. Pour in enough water to cover the rice by about 1 cm/½ inch. Add salt and bring to the boil. As soon as the water boils, cover the saucepan, reduce the heat as low as possible and cook for 10 minutes. Remove from the heat and leave to stand for a further 10 minutes. Do not lift the lid while cooking. Leave until cold, then stir with a fork.

Heat a wok, add the oil and when hot, add the smoked bacon. Stir-fry for 1 minute before adding the garlic and ginger, then stir-fry for a further 30 seconds.

Add the cooked rice and peas to the wok. Stir-fry over a high heat for 5 minutes.

Add the eggs and the beansprouts and continue to stir-fry for a further 2 minutes until the eggs have set. Season to taste with salt and pepper. Spoon the mixture onto a serving plate and garnish with the peanuts and spring onions. Serve hot or cold.

*Try this:* FOR AN ALTERNATIVE: 162  FOR A LIGHT BITE: 74

# Vegetables

# Warm Noodle Salad with Sesame & Peanut Dressing

**SERVES 4-6**

125 g/4 oz smooth
    peanut butter
6 tbsp sesame oil
3 tbsp light soy sauce
2 tbsp red wine vinegar
1 tbsp freshly grated
    root ginger

2 tbsp double cream
250 g pack Chinese fine
    egg noodles
125 g/4 oz beansprouts
225 g/8 oz baby sweetcorn
125 g/4 oz carrots, peeled
    and cut into matchsticks

125 g/4 oz mangetout
125 g/4 oz cucumber, cut
    into thin strips
3 spring onions, trimmed
    and finely shredded

Place the peanut butter, 4 tablespoons of the sesame oil, the soy sauce, vinegar and ginger in a food processor. Blend until smooth, then stir in 75 ml/3 fl oz hot water and blend again. Pour in the cream, blend briefly until smooth. Pour the dressing into a jug and reserve.

Bring a saucepan of lightly salted water to the boil, add the noodles and beansprouts and cook for 4 minutes or according to the packet instructions. Drain, rinse under cold running water and drain again. Stir in the remaining sesame oil and keep warm.

Bring a saucepan of lightly salted water to the boil and add the baby sweetcorn, carrots and mangetout and cook for 3–4 minutes, or until just tender but still crisp. Drain and cut the mangetout in half. Slice the baby sweetcorn (if very large) into 2–3 pieces and arrange on a warmed serving dish with the noodles. Add the cucumber strips and spring onions. Spoon over a little of the dressing and serve immediately with the remaining dressing.

*Try this:* FOR AN ALTERNATIVE: 302  FOR A LIGHT BITE: 66

# Chinese Egg Fried Rice

**SERVES 4**

250 g/9 oz long-grain rice
1 tbsp dark sesame oil
2 large eggs
1 tbsp sunflower oil
2 garlic cloves, peeled
  and crushed
2.5 cm/1 inch piece fresh
  root ginger, peeled

and grated
1 carrot, peeled and cut
  into matchsticks
125 g/4 oz mangetout,
  halved
220 g can water chestnuts,
  drained and halved
1 yellow pepper, deseeded

and diced
4 spring onions, trimmed
  and finely shredded
2 tbsp light soy sauce
½ tsp paprika
salt and freshly ground
  black pepper

Bring a saucepan of lightly salted water to the boil, add the rice and cook for 15 minutes or according to the packet instructions. Drain and leave to cool.

Heat a wok or large frying pan and add the sesame oil. Beat the eggs in a small bowl and pour into the hot wok. Using a fork, draw the egg in from the sides of the pan to the centre until it sets, then turn over and cook the other side. When set and golden turn out on to a board. Leave to cool, then cut into very thin strips.

Wipe the wok clean with absorbent kitchen paper, return to the heat and add the sunflower oil. When hot add the garlic and ginger and stir-fry for 30 seconds. Add the remaining vegetables and continue to stir-fry for 3–4 minutes, or until tender but still crisp.

Stir the reserved cooked rice into the wok with the soy sauce and paprika and season to taste with salt and pepper. Fold in the cooked egg strips and heat through. Tip into a warmed serving dish and serve immediately.

*Try this:* FOR AN ALTERNATIVE: 162   FOR A LIGHT BITE: 22

# Vegetable Tempura

**SERVES 4-6**

125 g/4 oz rice flour
75 g/3 oz plain flour
4 tsp baking powder
1 tbsp dried mustard
   powder
2 tsp semolina
salt and freshly ground

black pepper
300 ml/½ pint groundnut oil
125 g/4 oz courgette,
   trimmed and thickly sliced
125 g/4 oz mangetout
125 g/4 oz baby sweetcorn
4 small red onions, peeled

and quartered
1 large red pepper, deseeded
   and cut into 2.5 cm/1 inch
   wide strips
light soy sauce, to serve

Sift the rice flour and the plain flour into a large bowl, then sift in the baking powder and dried mustard powder.

Stir the semolina into the flour mixture and season to taste with salt and pepper. Gradually beat in 300 ml/½ pint cold water to produce a thin coating batter. Leave to stand at room temperature for 30 minutes.

Heat a wok or large frying pan, add the oil and heat to 180°C/350°F. Working in batches and using a slotted spoon, dip the vegetables in the batter until well coated, then drop them carefully into the hot oil. Cook each batch for 2–3 minutes or until golden. Drain on absorbent kitchen paper and keep warm while cooking the remaining batches.

Transfer the vegetables to a warmed serving platter and serve immediately with the light soy sauce to use as a dipping sauce.

*Try this:* FOR AN ALTERNATIVE: 304  FOR A LIGHT BITE: 52

# Thai–style Cauliflower & Potato Curry

**SERVES 4**

450 g/1 lb new potatoes, peeled and halved or quartered
350 g/12 oz cauliflower florets
3 garlic cloves, peeled and crushed
1 onion, peeled and finely chopped

40 g/1½ oz ground almonds
1 tsp ground coriander
½ tsp ground cumin
½ tsp turmeric
3 tbsp groundnut oil
salt and freshly ground black pepper
50 g/2 oz creamed coconut, broken into small pieces

200 ml/7 fl oz vegetable stock
1 tbsp mango chutney
sprigs of fresh coriander, to garnish
freshly cooked long-grain rice, to serve

Bring a saucepan of lightly salted water to the boil, add the potatoes and cook for 15 minutes or until just tender. Drain and leave to cool. Boil the cauliflower for 2 minutes, then drain and refresh under cold running water. Drain again and reserve.

Meanwhile, blend the garlic, onion, ground almonds and spices with 2 tablespoons of the oil and salt and pepper to taste in a food processor until a smooth paste is formed. Heat a wok, add the remaining oil and when hot, add the spice paste and cook for 3–4 minutes, stirring continuously.

Dissolve the creamed coconut in 6 tablespoons of boiling water and add to the wok. Pour in the stock, cook for 2–3 minutes, then stir in the cooked potatoes and cauliflower.

Stir in the mango chutney and heat through for 3–4 minutes or until piping hot. Tip into a warmed serving dish, garnish with sprigs of fresh coriander and serve immediately with freshly cooked rice.

*Try this:* FOR AN ALTERNATIVE: 322   FOR A LIGHT BITE: 58

# Cooked Vegetable Salad with Satay Sauce

**SERVES 4**

125 ml/4 fl oz groundnut oil
225 g/8 oz unsalted peanuts
1 onion, peeled and finely chopped
1 garlic clove, peeled and crushed
½ tsp chilli powder
1 tsp ground coriander
½ tsp ground cumin
½ tsp sugar

1 tbsp dark soy sauce
2 tbsp fresh lemon juice
2 tbsp light olive oil
salt and freshly ground black pepper
125 g/4 oz French green beans, trimmed and halved
125 g/4 oz carrots
125 g/4 oz cauliflower florets

125 g/4 oz broccoli florets
125 g/4 oz Chinese leaves or pak choi, trimmed and shredded
125 g/4 oz beansprouts
1 tbsp sesame oil

To garnish:
sprigs of fresh watercress
cucumber, cut into slivers

Heat a wok, add the oil, and when hot, add the peanuts and stir-fry for 3–4 minutes. Drain on absorbent kitchen paper and leave to cool. Blend in a food processor to a fine powder.

Place the onion and garlic, with the spices, sugar, soy sauce, lemon juice and olive oil in a food processor. Season to taste with salt and pepper, then process into a paste. Transfer to a wok and stir-fry for 3–4 minutes.

Stir 600 ml/1 pint hot water into the paste and bring to the boil. Add the ground peanuts and simmer gently for 5–6 minutes or until the mixture thickens. Reserve the satay sauce.

Cook in batches in lightly salted boiling water. Cook the French beans, carrots, cauliflower and broccoli for 3–4 minutes, and the Chinese leaves or pak choi and beansprouts for 2 minutes. Drain each batch, drizzle over the sesame oil and arrange on a large warmed serving dish. Garnish with watercress sprigs and cucumber. Serve with the satay sauce.

*Try this:* FOR AN ALTERNATIVE: 332  FOR A LIGHT BITE: 32

# Mixed Vegetables Stir Fry

**SERVES 4**

2 tbsp groundnut oil
4 garlic cloves, peeled and
    finely sliced
2.5 cm/1 inch piece fresh
    root ginger, peeled and
    finely sliced
75 g/3 oz broccoli florets

50 g/2 oz mangetout, trimmed
75 g/3 oz carrots, peeled and
    cut into matchsticks
1 green pepper, deseeded
    and cut into strips
1 red pepper, deseeded and
    cut into strips

1 tbsp soy sauce
1 tbsp hoisin sauce
1 tsp sugar
salt and freshly ground
    black pepper
4 spring onions, trimmed
    and shredded, to garnish

Heat a wok, add the oil and when hot, add the garlic and ginger slices and stir-fry for 1 minute.

Add the broccoli florets to the wok, stir-fry for 1 minute, then add the mangetout, carrots and the green and red peppers and stir-fry for a further 3–4 minutes, or until tender but still crisp.

Blend the soy sauce, hoisin sauce and sugar in a small bowl. Stir well, season to taste with salt and pepper and pour into the wok. Transfer the vegetables to a warmed serving dish. Garnish with shredded spring onions and serve immediately with a selection of other Thai dishes.

*Try this:* FOR AN ALTERNATIVE: 362   FOR A LIGHT BITE: 52

# Thai Stuffed Eggs with Spinach & Sesame Seeds

**MAKES 8**

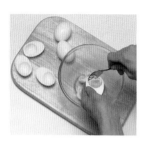

4 large eggs
salt and freshly ground
    black pepper
225 g/8 oz baby spinach
2 garlic cloves, peeled
    and crushed

1 tbsp spring onions,
    trimmed and finely
    chopped
1 tbsp sesame seeds
75 g/3 oz plain flour
1 tbsp light olive oil

300 ml/½ pint vegetable oil
    for frying
sliced red chilli, to garnish
snipped fresh chives,
    to garnish

Bring a small saucepan of water to the boil, add the eggs, bring back to the boil and cook for 6–7 minutes. Plunge into cold water, then shell and cut in half lengthways. Using a teaspoon, remove the yolks and place in a bowl. Reserve the whites.

Place 1 teaspoon of water and ½ teaspoon of salt in a saucepan, add the spinach and cook until tender and wilted. Drain, squeeze out the excess moisture and chop. Mix with the egg yolk, then stir in the garlic, spring onions and sesame seeds. Season to taste with salt and pepper. Fill the egg shells with the mixture, smoothing into a mound.

Place the flour in a bowl with the olive oil, a large pinch of salt and 125 ml/4 fl oz warm water. Beat together to make completely smooth batter.

Heat a wok, add the vegetable oil and heat to 180°C/350°F. Dip the stuffed eggs in the batter, allowing any excess batter to drip back into the bowl, and deep-fry in batches for 3–4 minutes or until golden brown. Place the eggs in the wok filled side down first, then turn over to finish cooking. Remove from the wok with a slotted spoon and drain on absorbent kitchen paper. Serve hot or cold garnished with snipped chives and chilli rings.

*Try this:* FOR AN ALTERNATIVE: 230  FOR A LIGHT BITE: 64

# Savoury Wontons

**MAKES 15**

125 g/4 oz filo pastry or
   wonton skins
15 whole chive leaves
225 g/8 oz spinach
25 g/1 oz butter
½ tsp salt
225 g/8 oz mushrooms, wiped

and roughly chopped
1 garlic clove, peeled
   and crushed
1–2 tbsp dark soy sauce
2.5 cm/1 inch piece fresh
   root ginger, peeled
   and grated

salt and freshly ground
   black pepper
1 small egg, beaten
300 ml/½ pint groundnut oil
   for deep-frying
spring onion curls, to garnish
radish roses, to garnish

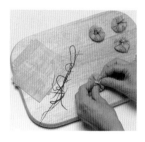

Cut the filo pastry or wonton skins into 12.5 cm/5 inch squares, stack and cover with clingfilm. Chill in the refrigerator while preparing the filling. Blanch the chive leaves in boiling water for 1 minute, drain and reserve.

Melt the butter in a saucepan, add the spinach and salt and cook for 2–3 minutes or until wilted. Add the mushrooms and garlic and cook for 2–3 minutes or until tender.

Transfer the spinach and mushroom mixture to a bowl. Stir in the soy sauce and ginger. Season to taste with salt and pepper.

Place a small spoonful of the spinach and mushroom mixture on to a pastry or wonton square and brush the edges with beaten egg. Gather up the 4 corners to make a little bag and tie with a chive leaf. Make up the remainder of the wontons.

Heat a wok, add the oil and heat to 180°C/350°F. Deep-fry the wontons in batches for 2–3 minutes, or until golden and crisp. Drain on absorbent kitchen paper and serve immediately, garnished with spring onion curls and radish roses.

    *Try this:* FOR AN ALTERNATIVE: 104  FOR A LIGHT BITE: 30

# Corn Fritters with Hot & Spicy Relish

**MAKES 16–20**

325 g can sweetcorn
   kernels, drained
1 onion, peeled and very
   finely chopped
1 spring onion, trimmed and
   very finely chopped
½ tsp chilli powder
1 tsp ground coriander
4 tbsp plain flour

1 tsp baking powder
1 medium egg
salt and freshly ground black
   pepper
300 ml/½ pint groundnut oil
sprigs of fresh coriander,
   to garnish

**For the spicy relish:**
3 tbsp sunflower oil
1 onion, peeled and very
   finely chopped
¼ tsp dried crushed chillies
2 garlic cloves, peeled
   and crushed
2 tbsp plum sauce

Make the relish. Heat a wok, add the sunflower oil and when hot, add the onion and stir-fry for 3–4 minutes or until softened. Add the chillies and garlic, stir-fry for 1 minute, then leave to cool slightly. Stir in the plum sauce, transfer to a food processor and blend until the consistency of chutney. Reserve.

Place the sweetcorn into a food processor and blend briefly until just mashed. Transfer to a bowl with the onions, chilli powder, coriander, flour, baking powder and egg. Season to taste with salt and pepper and mix together.

Heat a wok, add the oil and heat to 180˚C/350˚F Working in batches, drop a few spoonfuls of the sweetcorn mixture into the oil and deep-fry for 3–4 minutes, or until golden and crispy, turning occasionally. Using a slotted spoon, remove and drain on absorbent kitchen paper. Arrange on a warmed serving platter, garnish with sprigs of coriander and serve immediately with the relish.

*Try this:* FOR AN ALTERNATIVE:286 FOR A LIGHT BITE: 34

# Chinese Leaves with Sweet-&-Sour Sauce

**SERVES 4**

1 head Chinese leaves
200 g pack pak choi
1 tbsp cornflour
1 tbsp soy sauce

2 tbsp brown sugar
3 tbsp red wine vinegar
3 tbsp orange juice
2 tbsp tomato purée

3 tbsp sunflower oil
15 g/½ oz butter
1 tsp salt
2 tbsp toasted sesame seeds

Discard any tough outer leaves and stalks from the Chinese leaves and pak choi and wash well. Drain thoroughly and pat dry with absorbent kitchen paper. Shred the Chinese leaves and pak choi lengthways. Reserve.

In a small bowl, blend the cornflour with 4 tablespoons of water. Add the soy sauce, sugar, vinegar, orange juice and tomato purée and stir until blended thoroughly.

Pour the sauce into a small saucepan and bring to the boil. Simmer gently for 2–3 minutes, or until the sauce is thickened and smooth.

Meanwhile, heat a wok or large frying pan and add the sunflower oil and butter. When melted, add the prepared Chinese leaves and pak choi, sprinkle with the salt and stir-fry for 2 minutes. Reduce the heat and cook gently for a further 1–2 minutes or until tender.

Transfer the Chinese leaves and pak choi to a warmed serving platter and drizzle over the warm sauce. Sprinkle with the toasted sesame seeds and serve immediately.

*Try this:* FOR AN ALTERNATIVE: 318  FOR A LIGHT BITE: 64

# Bean & Cashew Stir Fry

**SERVES 4**

3 tbsp sunflower oil
1 onion, peeled and
   finely chopped
1 celery stalk, trimmed
   and chopped
2.5 cm/1 inch piece fresh
   root ginger, peeled
   and grated
2 garlic cloves, peeled
   and crushed
1 red chilli, deseeded
   and finely chopped
175 g/6 oz fine French beans,
   trimmed and halved
175 g/6 oz mangetout, sliced
   diagonally into 3
75 g/3 oz unsalted
   cashew nuts
1 tsp brown sugar
125 ml/4 fl oz vegetable stock
2 tbsp dry sherry
1 tbsp light soy sauce
1 tsp red wine vinegar
salt and freshly ground
   black pepper
freshly chopped coriander,
   to garnish

Heat a wok or large frying pan, add the oil and when hot, add the onion and celery and stir-fry gently for 3–4 minutes or until softened.

Add the ginger, garlic and chilli to the wok and stir-fry for 30 seconds. Stir in the French beans and mangetout together with the cashew nuts and continue to stir-fry for 1–2 minutes, or until the nuts are golden brown.

Dissolve the sugar in the stock, then blend with the sherry, soy sauce and vinegar. Stir into the bean mixture and bring to the boil. Simmer gently, stirring occasionally for 3–4 minutes, or until the beans and mangetout are tender but still crisp and the sauce has thickened slightly. Season to taste with salt and pepper. Transfer to a warmed serving bowl or spoon on to individual plates. Sprinkle with freshly chopped coriander and serve immediately.

*Try this:* FOR AN ALTERNATIVE: 172  FOR A LIGHT BITE: 52

# Fried Rice with Bamboo Shoots & Ginger

**SERVES 4**

4 tbsp sunflower oil
1 onion, peeled and
    finely chopped
225 g/8 oz long-grain rice
3 garlic cloves, peeled and
    cut into slivers
2.5 cm/1 inch piece fresh
    root ginger, peeled

and grated
3 spring onions, trimmed
    and chopped
450 ml/¾ pint vegetable stock
125 g/4 oz button
    mushrooms, wiped
    and halved
75 g/3 oz frozen peas, thawed

2 tbsp light soy sauce
500 g can bamboo shoots,
    drained and thinly sliced
salt and freshly ground
    black pepper
cayenne pepper, to taste
fresh coriander leaves,
    to garnish

Heat a wok, add the oil and when hot, add the onion and cook gently for 3–4 minutes, then add the long-grain rice and cook for 3–4 minutes or until golden, stirring frequently.

Add the garlic, ginger and chopped spring onions to the wok and stir well. Pour the chicken stock into a small saucepan and bring to the boil. Carefully ladle the hot stock into the wok, stir well, then simmer gently for 10 minutes or until most of the liquid has been absorbed.

Stir the button mushrooms, peas and soy sauce into the wok and continue to cook for a further 5 minutes, or until the rice is tender, adding a little extra stock if necessary.

Add the bamboo shoots to the wok and carefully stir in. Season to taste with salt, pepper and cayenne pepper. Cook for 2–3 minutes or until heated through. Tip on to a warmed serving dish, garnish with coriander leaves and serve immediately.

*Try this:* FOR AN ALTERNATIVE: 360   FOR A LIGHT BITE: 62

# Thai Curry with Tofu

**SERVES 4**

750 ml/1¼ pints coconut milk
700 g/1½ lb tofu, drained and
  cut into small cubes
salt and freshly ground
  black pepper
4 garlic cloves, peeled
  and chopped
1 large onion, peeled and
  cut into wedges

1 tsp crushed dried chillies
grated rind of 1 lemon
2.5 cm/1 inch piece fresh
  root ginger, peeled
  and grated
1 tbsp ground coriander
1 tsp ground cumin
1 tsp turmeric
2 tbsp light soy sauce

1 tsp cornflour
Thai fragrant rice, to serve
2 red chillies, deseeded and
  cut into rings, to garnish
1 tbsp freshly chopped
  coriander, to garnish
lemon wedges, to garnish

Pour 600 ml/1 pint of the coconut milk into a saucepan and bring to the boil. Add the tofu, season to taste with salt and pepper and simmer gently for 10 minutes. Using a slotted spoon, remove the tofu and place on a plate. Reserve the coconut milk.

Place the garlic, onion, dried chillies, lemon rind, ginger, spices and soy sauce in a blender or food processor and blend until a smooth paste is formed. Pour the remaining 150 ml/¼ pint coconut milk into a clean saucepan and whisk in the spicy paste. Cook, stirring continuously, for 15 minutes, or until the curry sauce is very thick.

Gradually whisk the reserved coconut milk into the curry and heat to simmering point. Add the cooked tofu and cook for 5–10 minutes. Blend the cornflour with 1 tablespoon of cold water and stir into the curry. Cook until thickened. Turn into a warmed serving dish and garnish with chilli, lemon wedges and coriander. Serve immediately with Thai fragrant rice.

*Try this:* FOR AN ALTERNATIVE: 314 FOR A LIGHT BITE: 22

# Chinese Omelette

**SERVES 1**

50 g/2 oz beansprouts
50 g/2 oz carrots, peeled and
   cut into matchsticks
1 cm/½ inch piece fresh root
   ginger, peeled and grated

1 tsp soy sauce
2 large eggs
salt and freshly ground
   black pepper
1 tbsp dark sesame oil

tossed green salad, to serve
Special Fried Rice, (see page
   162) soy sauce, to serve

Lightly rinse the beansprouts, then place in the top of a bamboo steamer with the carrots. Add the grated ginger and soy sauce. Set the steamer over a pan or wok half-filled with gently simmering water and steam for 10 minutes, or until the vegetables are tender but still crisp. Reserve and keep warm.

Whisk the eggs in a bowl until frothy and season to taste with salt and pepper. Heat a 20.5 cm/8 inch omelette or frying pan, add the sesame oil and when very hot, pour in the beaten eggs. Whisk the eggs around with a fork, then allow them to cook and start to set. When the top surface starts to bubble, tilt the edges to allow the uncooked egg to run underneath.

Spoon the beansprout and carrot mixture over the top of the omelette and allow it to cook a little longer. When it has set, slide the omelette on to a warmed serving dish and carefully roll up. Serve immediately with a tossed green salad, special fried rice and extra soy sauce.

*Try this:* FOR AN ALTERNATIVE: 230 FOR A LIGHT BITE: 24

# Crispy Pancake Rolls

**MAKES 8**

250 g/9 oz plain flour
pinch of salt
1 medium egg
4 tsp sunflower oil
2 tbsp light olive oil
2 cm/¾ inch piece fresh root
ginger, peeled and grated
1 garlic clove, peeled

and crushed
225 g/8 oz tofu, drained and
cut into small dice
2 tbsp soy sauce
1 tbsp dry sherry
175 g/6 oz button
mushrooms, wiped
and chopped

1 celery stalk, trimmed and
finely chopped
2 spring onions, trimmed
and finely chopped
2 tbsp groundnut oil
fresh coriander sprig and
sliced spring onion,
to garnish

Sift 225 g/8 oz of the flour with the salt into a large bowl, make a well in the centre and drop in the egg. Beat to form a smooth, thin batter, gradually adding 300 ml/½ pint of water and drawing in the flour from the sides of the bowl. Mix the remaining flour with 1–2 tablespoons of water to make a thick paste. Reserve.

Heat a little sunflower oil in a 20.5 cm/8 inch omelette or frying pan and pour in 2 tablespoons of the batter. Cook for 1–2 minutes, flip over and cook for a further 1–2 minutes, or until firm. Slide from the pan and keep warm. Make more pancakes with the remaining batter.

Heat a wok or large frying pan, add the olive oil and when hot, add the ginger, garlic and tofu, stir-fry for 30 seconds, then pour in the soy sauce and sherry. Add the mushrooms, celery and spring onions. Stir-fry for 1–2 minutes, then remove from the wok and leave to cool.

Place a little filling in the centre of each pancake. Brush the edges, with the flour paste, fold in the edges, then roll up into parcels. Heat the groundnut oil to 180°C/350°F. in the wok. Fry the pancake rolls for 2–3 minutes or until golden. Serve immediately, garnished with chopped spring onions and a sprig of coriander.

*Try this:* FOR AN ALTERNATIVE: 278 FOR A LIGHT BITE: 52

# Vegetables in Coconut Milk with Rice Noodles

**SERVES 4**

75 g/3 oz creamed coconut
1 tsp salt
2 tbsp sunflower oil
2 garlic cloves, peeled and finely chopped
2 red peppers, deseeded and cut into thin strips
2.5 cm/1 inch piece of fresh root ginger, peeled and cut into thin strips
125 g/4 oz baby sweetcorn
2 tsp cornflour
2 medium ripe but still firm avocados
1 small Cos lettuce, cut into thick strips
freshly cooked rice noodles, to serve

Roughly chop the creamed coconut, place in a bowl with the salt, then pour over 600 ml/1 pint of boiling water. Stir until the coconut has dissolved completely and reserve.

Heat a wok or large frying pan, add the oil and when hot, add the chopped garlic, sliced peppers and ginger. Cook for 30 seconds, then cover and cook very gently for 10 minutes or until the peppers are soft.

Pour in the reserved coconut milk and bring to the boil. Stir in the baby sweetcorn, cover and simmer for 5 minutes. Blend the cornflour with 2 teaspoons of water, pour into the wok and cook, stirring, for 2 minutes or until thickened slightly.

Cut the avocados in half, peel, remove the stone and slice. Add to the wok with the lettuce strips and stir until well mixed and heated through. Serve immediately on a bed of rice noodles.

*Try this:* FOR AN ALTERNATIVE: 332 FOR A LIGHT BITE: 22

# Entertaining & Desserts

# Sweet-&-Sour Shredded Beef

**SERVES 4**

350 g/12 oz rump steak
1 tsp sesame oil
2 tbsp Chinese rice wine or
   sweet sherry
2 tbsp dark soy sauce
1 tsp cornflour
4 tbsp pineapple juice
2 tsp soft light brown sugar

1 tsp sherry vinegar
salt and freshly ground
   black pepper
2 tbsp groundnut oil
2 medium carrots, peeled
   and cut into matchsticks
125 g/4 oz mangetout peas,
   trimmed and cut into

   matchsticks
1 bunch spring onions,
   trimmed and shredded
2 garlic cloves, peeled
   and crushed
1 tbsp toasted sesame seeds
freshly cooked Thai fragrant
   rice, to serve

Cut the steak across the grain into thin strips. Put in a bowl with the sesame oil,
1 tablespoon of the Chinese rice wine or sherry and 1 tablespoon of the soy sauce. Mix well,
cover and leave to marinate in the refrigerator for 30 minutes.

In a small bowl, blend together the cornflour with the remaining Chinese rice wine or sherry,
then stir in the pineapple juice, remaining soy sauce, sugar and vinegar. Season with a little
salt and pepper and reserve.

Heat a wok until hot, add 1 tablespoon of the oil, then drain the beef, reserving the marinade,
and stir-fry for 1–2 minutes, or until browned. Remove from the wok and reserve.

Add the remaining oil to the wok then add the carrots and stir-fry for 1 minute, then add the
mangetout peas and spring onions and stir-fry for a further 1 minute.

Return the beef to the wok with the sauce, reserved marinade and garlic. Continue cooking for
1 minute or until the vegetables are tender and the sauce is bubbling. Turn the stir-fry into a
warmed serving dish, sprinkle with toasted sesame seeds and serve immediately with the
Thai fragrant rice.

   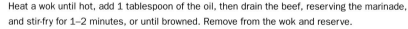 *Try this:* FOR AN ALTERNATIVE: 186   FOR A LIGHT BITE: 80

# Kung-pao Lamb

**SERVES 4**

450 g/1 lb lamb fillet
2 tbsp soy sauce
2 tbsp Chinese rice wine or
    dry sherry
2 tbsp sunflower oil
2 tsp sesame oil
50 g/2 oz unsalted peanuts
1 garlic clove, peeled
    and crushed

2.5 cm/1 inch piece
    fresh root ginger,
    finely chopped
1 red chilli, deseeded and
    finely chopped
1 small green pepper,
    deseeded and diced
6 spring onions, trimmed
    and diagonally sliced

125 ml/4 fl oz lamb or
    vegetable stock
1 tsp red wine vinegar
1 tsp soft light brown sugar
2 tsp cornflour
plain boiled or steamed
    white rice, to serve

Wrap the lamb in baking parchment paper and place in the freezer for about 30 minutes until stiff. Cut the meat across the grain into paper-thin slices. Put in a shallow bowl, add 2 teaspoons of the soy sauce and all the Chinese rice wine or sherry and leave to marinate in the refrigerator for 15 minutes.

Heat a wok or frying pan until hot, add the sunflower oil and swirl it around to coat the sides. Add the lamb and stir-fry for about 1 minute until lightly browned. Remove from the wok or pan and reserve, leaving any juices behind.

Add the sesame oil to the wok or pan and stir-fry the peanuts, garlic, ginger, chilli, green pepper and spring onions for 1–2 minutes, or until the nuts are golden. Return the lamb with the remaining soy sauce, stock, vinegar and sugar.

Blend the cornflour with 1 tablespoon of water. Stir in and cook the mixture for 1–2 minutes, or until the vegetables are tender and the sauce has thickened. Serve immediately with plain boiled or steamed white rice.

*Try this:* FOR AN ALTERNATIVE: 176   FOR A LIGHT BITE: 76

# Chicken & Lamb Satay

**MAKES 16**

225 g/8 oz skinless,
  boneless chicken
225 g/8 oz lean lamb

**For the marinade:**
1 small onion, peeled and
  finely chopped
2 garlic cloves, peeled
  and crushed
2.5 cm/1 inch piece fresh
  root ginger, peeled

  and grated
4 tbsp soy sauce
1 tsp ground coriander
2 tsp dark brown sugar
2 tbsp lime juice
1 tbsp vegetable oil

**For the peanut sauce:**
300 ml/½ pint coconut milk
4 tbsp crunchy peanut butter
1 tbsp Thai fish sauce

1 tsp lime juice
1 tbsp chilli powder
1 tbsp brown sugar
salt and freshly ground
  black pepper

sprigs of fresh coriander,
  to garnish
lime wedges, to garnish

Preheat the grill just before cooking. Soak the bamboo skewers for 30 minutes before required. Cut the chicken and lamb into thin strips, about 7.5 cm/3 inches long and place in 2 shallow dishes. Blend all the marinade ingredients together, then pour half over the chicken and half over the lamb. Stir until lightly coated, then cover with clingfilm and leave to marinate in the refrigerator for at least 2 hours, turning occasionally.

Remove the chicken and lamb from the marinade and thread on to the skewers. Reserve the marinade. Cook under the preheated grill for 8–10 minutes or until cooked, turning and brushing with the marinade.

Meanwhile, make the peanut sauce. Blend the coconut milk with the peanut butter, fish sauce, lime juice, chilli powder and sugar. Pour into a saucepan and cook gently for 5 minutes, stirring occasionally, then season to taste with salt and pepper. Garnish with coriander sprigs and lime wedges and serve the satays with the prepared sauce.

*Try this:* FOR AN ALTERNATIVE: 176  FOR A LIGHT BITE: 32

# Szechuan Sesame Chicken

**SERVES 4**

1 medium egg white
pinch of salt
2 tsp cornflour
450 g/1 lb boneless, skinless
    chicken breast, cut into
    7.5 cm/3 inch strips
300 ml/½ pint groundnut oil

1 tbsp sesame seeds
2 tsp dark soy sauce
2 tsp cider vinegar
2 tsp chilli bean sauce
2 tsp sesame oil
2 tsp sugar
1 tbsp Chinese rice wine

1 tsp whole Szechuan
    peppercorns, roasted
2 tbsp spring onion,
    trimmed and
    finely chopped
mixed salad, to serve

Beat the egg white with a pinch of salt and the cornflour, pour into a shallow dish and add the chicken strips. Turn to coat, cover with clingfilm and leave in the refrigerator for 20 minutes.

Heat a wok, add the groundnut oil and when hot, add the chicken pieces and stir-fry for 2 minutes or until the chicken turns white. Using a slotted spoon, remove the chicken and drain on absorbent kitchen paper. Pour off the oil and reserve 1 tablespoon of the oil. Wipe the wok clean.

Reheat the wok, add 1 tablespoon of the groundnut oil with the sesame seeds and stir-fry for 30 seconds, or until golden. Stir in the dark soy sauce, cider vinegar, chilli bean sauce, sesame oil, sugar, Chinese rice wine, Szechuan peppercorns and the spring onions. Bring to the boil.

Return the chicken to the wok and stir-fry for 2 minutes, making sure that the chicken is coated evenly with the sauce and sesame seeds. Turn into a warmed serving dish and serve immediately with a mixed salad.

*Try this:* FOR AN ALTERNATIVE: 208   FOR A LIGHT BITE: 32

# Turkey with Oriental Mushrooms

**SERVES 4**

15 g/½ oz dried Chinese mushrooms
450 g/1 lb turkey breast steaks
150 ml/¼ pint turkey or chicken stock
2 tbsp groundnut oil
1 red pepper, deseeded and sliced
225 g/8 oz sugar snap peas, trimmed
125 g/4 oz shiitake mushrooms, wiped and halved
125 g/4 oz oyster mushrooms, wiped and halved
2 tbsp yellow bean sauce
2 tbsp soy sauce
1 tbsp hot chilli sauce
freshly cooked noodles, to serve

Place the dried mushrooms in a small bowl, cover with almost boiling water and leave for 20–30 minutes. Drain and discard any woody stems from the mushrooms. Cut the turkey and into thin strips.

Pour the turkey or chicken stock into a wok or large frying pan and bring to the boil. Add the turkey and cook gently for 3 minutes, or until the turkey is sealed completely, then using a slotted spoon, remove from the wok and reserve. Discard any stock.

Wipe the wok clean and reheat, then add the oil. When the oil is almost smoking, add the drained turkey and stir-fry for 2 minutes.

Add the drained mushrooms to the wok with the red pepper, the sugar snap peas and the shiitake and oyster mushrooms. Stir-fry for 2 minutes, then add the yellow bean, soy and hot chilli sauces.

Stir-fry the mixture for 1–2 minutes more, or until the turkey is cooked thoroughly and the vegetables are cooked but still retain a bite. Turn into a warmed serving dish and serve immediately with freshly cooked noodles.

*Try this:* FOR AN ALTERNATIVE: 260   FOR A LIGHT BITE: 64

# Crispy Aromatic Duck

**SERVES 4–6**

2 tbsp Chinese five
  spice powder
75 g/3 oz Szechuan
  peppercorns, lightly crushed
25 g/1 oz whole black
  peppercorns, lightly crushed
3 tbsp cumin seeds,
  lightly crushed
200 g/7 oz rock salt

2.7 kg/6 lb oven-ready duck
7.5 cm/3 inch piece fresh
  root ginger, peeled and
  cut into 6 slices
6 spring onions, trimmed
  and cut into 7.5 cm/
  3 inch lengths
cornflour for dusting
1.1 litres/2 pints

groundnut oil
warm Chinese pancakes,
  to serve
spring onion, cut into
  shreds, to serve
cucumber, cut into slices
  lengthways, to serve
hoisin sauce, to serve

Mix together the Chinese five spice powder, Szechuan and black peppercorns, cumin seeds and salt. Rub the duck inside and out with the spice mixture. Wrap the duck with clingfilm and place in the refrigerator for 24 hours. Brush any loose spices from the duck. Place the ginger and spring onions into the duck cavity and put the duck on a heatproof plate.

Place a wire rack in a wok and pour in boiling water to a depth of 5 cm/2 inches. Lower the duck and plate on to the rack and cover. Steam gently for 2 hours or until the duck is cooked through, pouring off excess fat from time to time and adding more water, if necessary. Remove the duck, pour off all the liquid and discard the ginger and spring onions. Leave the duck in a cool place for 2 hours, or until it has dried and cooled.

Cut the duck into quarters and dust lightly with cornflour. Heat the oil in a wok or deep-fat fryer to 190°C/375°F, then deep-fry the duck quarters 2 at a time. Cook the breast for 8–10 minutes and the thighs and legs for 12–14 minutes, or until each piece is heated through. Drain on absorbent kitchen paper, then shred with a fork. Serve immediately with warm Chinese pancakes, spring onion shreds, cucumber slices and hoisin sauce.

*Try this:* FOR AN ALTERNATIVE: 218  FOR A LIGHT BITE: 80

# Honey–glazed Duck in Kumquat Sauce

**SERVES 4**

4 duck breast fillets
1 tbsp light soy sauce
1 tsp sesame oil
1 tbsp clear honey
3 tbsp brandy
1 tbsp sunflower oil

2 tbsp caster sugar
1 tbsp white wine vinegar
150 ml/¼ pint orange juice
125 g/4 oz kumquats,
    thinly sliced
2 tsp cornflour

salt and freshly ground
    black pepper
fresh watercress, to garnish
basmati and wild rice,
    to serve

Thinly slice the duck breasts and put in a shallow bowl. Mix together the soy sauce, sesame oil, honey and 1 tablespoon of brandy. Pour over the duck, stir well, cover and marinate in the refrigerator for at least 1 hour.

Heat a wok until hot, add the sunflower oil and swirl it round to coat the sides. Drain the duck, reserving the marinade, and stir-fry over a high heat for 2–3 minutes, or until browned. Remove from the wok; reserve.

Wipe the wok clean with absorbent kitchen paper. Add the sugar, vinegar and 1 tablespoon of water. Gently heat until the sugar dissolves, then boil until a rich golden colour. Pour in the orange juice, then the remaining brandy. Stir in the kumquat slices and simmer for 5 minutes.

Blend the cornflour with 1 tablespoon of cold water. Add to the wok and simmer for 2–3 minutes, stirring until thickened. Return the duck to the wok and cook gently for 1–2 minutes, or until warmed through. Season to taste with salt and pepper. Spoon onto warmed plates and garnish with fresh watercress leaves. Serve immediately with freshly cooked basmati and wild rice.

*Try this:* FOR AN ALTERNATIVE: 270   FOR A LIGHT BITE: 80

# Dim Sum Pork Parcels

## MAKES ABOUT 40

125 g/4 oz canned water
   chestnuts, drained and
   finely chopped
125 g/4 oz raw prawns,
   peeled, deveined and
   coarsely chopped
350 g/12 oz fresh pork mince
2 tbsp smoked bacon,
   finely chopped
1 tbsp light soy sauce, plus

extra, to serve
1 tsp dark soy sauce
1 tbsp Chinese rice wine
2 tbsp fresh root ginger,
   peeled and finely chopped
3 spring onions, trimmed
   and finely chopped
2 tsp sesame oil
1 medium egg white,
   lightly beaten

salt and freshly ground
   black pepper
2 tsp sugar
40 wonton skins, thawed
   if frozen
toasted sesame seeds,
   to garnish
soy sauce, to serve

Place the water chestnuts, prawns, pork mince and bacon in a bowl and mix together. Add the soy sauces, Chinese rice wine, ginger, chopped spring onion, sesame oil and egg white. Season to taste with salt and pepper, sprinkle in the sugar and mix the filling thoroughly.

Place a spoonful of filling in the centre of a wonton skin. Bring the sides up and press around the filling to make a basket shape. Flatten the base of the skin, so the wonton stands solid. The top should be wide open, exposing the filling.

Place the parcels on a heatproof plate, on a wire rack inside a wok or on the base of a muslin-lined bamboo steamer. Place over a wok, half-filled with boiling water, cover, then steam the parcels for about 20 minutes. Do this in 2 batches. Transfer to a warmed serving plate, sprinkle with toasted sesame seeds, drizzle with soy sauce and serve immediately.

*Try this:* FOR AN ALTERNATIVE: 178   FOR A LIGHT BITE: 70

# Pork with Tofu

**SERVES 4**

450 g/1 lb smoked firm
   tofu, drained
2 tbsp groundnut oil
3 garlic cloves, peeled
   and crushed
2.5 cm/1 inch piece fresh
   root ginger, peeled and
finely chopped
350 g/12 oz fresh pork mince
1 tbsp chilli powder
1 tsp sugar
2 tbsp Chinese rice wine
1 tbsp dark soy sauce
1 tbsp light soy sauce
2 tbsp yellow bean sauce
1 tsp Szechuan peppercorns
75 ml/3 fl oz chicken stock
spring onions, trimmed and
   finely sliced, to garnish
fried rice, to serve

Cut the tofu into 1 cm/½ inch cubes and place in a sieve to drain. Place the tofu on absorbent kitchen paper to dry thoroughly for another 10 minutes.

Heat the wok, add the groundnut oil and when hot, add the garlic and ginger. Stir-fry for a few seconds to flavour the oil, but not to colour the vegetables. Add the pork mince and stir-fry for 3 minutes, or until the pork is sealed and there are no lumps in the mince.

Add all the remaining ingredients except for the tofu. Bring the mixture to the boil, then reduce the heat to low. Add the tofu and mix it in gently, taking care not to break up the tofu chunks, but ensuring an even mixture of ingredients. Simmer, uncovered, for 15 minutes, or until the tofu is tender. Turn into a warmed serving dish, garnish with sliced spring onions and serve immediately with fried rice.

*Try this:* FOR AN ALTERNATIVE: 154   FOR A LIGHT BITE: 22

# Thai Green Fragrant Mussels

**SERVES 4**

2 kg/4½ lb fresh mussels
4 tbsp olive oil
2 garlic cloves, peeled and finely sliced
3 tbsp fresh root ginger, peeled and finely sliced
3 lemon grass stalks, outer leaves discarded and finely sliced
1–3 red or green chillies, deseeded and chopped
1 green pepper, deseeded and diced
5 spring onions, trimmed and finely sliced
3 tbsp freshly chopped coriander
1 tbsp sesame oil
juice of 3 limes
400 ml can coconut milk
warm crusty bread, to serve

Scrub the mussels under cold running water, removing any barnacles and beards. Discard any that have broken or damaged shells or are opened and do not close when tapped gently.

Heat a wok or large frying pan, add the oil and when hot, add the mussels. Shake gently and cook for 1 minute, then add the garlic, ginger, sliced lemon grass, chillies, green pepper, spring onions, 2 tablespoons of the chopped coriander and the sesame oil.

Stir-fry over a medium heat for 3–4 minutes, or until the mussels are cooked and have opened. Discard any mussels that remain unopened.

Pour the lime juice with the coconut milk into the wok and bring to the boil. Tip the mussels and the cooking liquor into warmed individual bowls. Sprinkle with the remaining chopped coriander and serve immediately with warm crusty bread.

*Try this:* FOR AN ALTERNATIVE: 362   FOR A LIGHT BITE: 26

# Ginger Lobster

**SERVES 4**

1 celery stalk, trimmed and finely chopped
1 onion, peeled and chopped
1 small leek, trimmed and chopped
10 black peppercorns
1 x 550 g/1¼ lb live lobster
25 g/1 oz butter
75 g/3 oz raw prawns, peeled and finely chopped

6 tbsp fish stock
50 g/2 oz fresh root ginger, peeled and cut into matchsticks
2 shallots, peeled and finely chopped
4 shiitake mushrooms, wiped and finely chopped
1 tsp green peppercorns, drained and crushed

2 tbsp oyster sauce
freshly ground black pepper
¼ tsp cornflour
sprigs of fresh coriander, to garnish
freshly cooked Thai rice and mixed shredded leek, celery, and red chilli, to serve

Place the celery, onion and leek in a large saucepan with the black peppercorns. Pour in 2 litres/3½ pints of hot water, bring to the boil and boil for 5 minutes, then immerse the lobster and boil for a further 8 minutes.

Remove the lobster. When cool enough to handle, sit it on its back. Using a sharp knife, halve the lobster neatly along its entire length. Remove and discard the intestinal vein from the tail, the stomach, (which lies near the head) and the inedible gills or dead man's fingers. Remove the meat from the shell and claws and cut into pieces.

Heat a wok or large frying pan, add the butter and when melted, add the raw prawns and fish stock. Stir-fry for 3 minutes or until the prawns change colour. Add the ginger, shallots, mushrooms, green peppercorns and oyster sauce. Season to taste with black pepper. Stir in the lobster. Stir-fry for 2–3 minutes.

Blend the cornflour with 1 teaspoon of water to form a thick paste, stir into the wok and cook, stirring, until the sauce thickens. Place the lobster on a warmed serving platter and tip the sauce over. Garnish and serve immediately.

*Try this:* FOR AN ALTERNATIVE: 126   FOR A LIGHT BITE: 60

# Sour-&-Spicy Prawn Soup

**SERVES 4**

50 g/2 oz rice noodles
25 g/1 oz Chinese dried
　mushrooms
4 spring onions, trimmed
2 small green chillies
3 tbsp freshly chopped
　coriander

600 ml/1 pint chicken stock
2.5 cm/1 inch piece fresh
　root ginger, peeled
　and grated
2 lemon grass stalks, outer
　leaves discarded and
　finely chopped

4 kaffir lime leaves
12 raw king prawns, peeled
　with tail shell left on
2 tbsp Thai fish sauce
2 tbsp lime juice
salt and freshly ground
　black pepper

Place the noodles in cold water and leave to soak while preparing the soup. Place the dried mushrooms in a small bowl, cover with almost boiling water and leave for 20–30 minutes. Drain, strain and reserve the soaking liquor and discard any woody stems from the mushrooms.

Finely shred the spring onions and place into a small bowl. Cover with ice cold water and refrigerate until required and the spring onions have curled.

Place the green chillies with 2 tablespoons of the chopped coriander in a pestle and mortar and pound to a paste. Reserve.

Pour the stock into a saucepan and bring gently to the boil. Stir in the ginger, lemon grass and lime leaves with the reserved mushrooms and their liquor. Return to the boil.

Drain the noodles, add to the soup with the prawns, Thai fish sauce and lime juice and then stir in the chilli and coriander paste. Bring to the boil, then simmer for 3 minutes. Stir in the remaining chopped coriander and season to taste with salt and pepper. Ladle into warmed bowls sprinkle with the spring onions curls and serve immediately.

*Try this:* FOR AN ALTERNATIVE: 110　FOR A LIGHT BITE: 58

# Royal Fried Rice

**SERVES 4**

450 g/1 lb Thai fragrant rice
2 large eggs
2 tsp sesame oil
salt and freshly ground
 black pepper
3 tbsp vegetable oil
1 red pepper, deseeded and
 finely diced

1 yellow pepper, deseeded
 and finely diced
1 green pepper, deseeded
 and finely diced
2 red onions, peeled
 and diced
125 g/4 oz sweetcorn kernels
125 g/4 oz cooked peeled

prawns, thawed if frozen
125 g/4 oz white crabmeat,
 drained if canned
¼ tsp sugar
2 tsp light soy sauce
radish roses, to garnish
freshly snipped and whole
 chive leaves, to garnish

Place the rice in a sieve, rinse with cold water, then drain. Place in a saucepan and add twice the volume of water, stirring briefly. Bring to the boil, cover and simmer gently for 15 minutes without further stirring. If the rice has fully absorbed the water while covered, add a little more water. Continue to simmer, uncovered, for another 5 minutes, or until the rice is fully cooked and the water has evaporated. Leave to cool.

Place the eggs, sesame oil and a pinch of salt in a small bowl. Using a fork, mix just to break the egg. Reserve.

Heat a wok and add 1 tablespoon of the vegetable oil. When very hot, stir-fry the peppers, onion and sweetcorn for 2 minutes or until the onion is soft. Remove the vegetables and reserve.

Clean the wok and add the remaining oil. When very hot, add the cold cooked rice and stir-fry for 3 minutes, or until it is heated through. Drizzle in the egg mixture and continue to stir-fry for 2–3 minutes or until the eggs have set. Add the prawns and crabmeat to the rice. Stir-fry for 1 minute. Season to taste with salt and pepper and add the sugar with the soy sauce. Stir to mix and spoon into a warmed serving dish. Garnish with a radish flower and sprinkle with freshly snipped and whole chives. Serve immediately.

*Try this:* FOR AN ALTERNATIVE: 310  FOR A LIGHT BITE: 74

# Stir-fried Greens

**SERVES 4**

450 g/1 lb Chinese leaves
225 g/8 oz pak choi
225 g/8 oz broccoli florets
1 tbsp sesame seeds
1 tbsp groundnut oil
1 tbsp fresh root ginger, peeled and finely chopped

3 garlic cloves, peeled and finely chopped
2 red chillies, deseeded and split in half
50 ml/2 fl oz chicken stock
2 tbsp Chinese rice wine
1 tbsp dark soy sauce

1 tsp light soy sauce
2 tsp black bean sauce
freshly ground black pepper
2 tsp sugar
1 tsp sesame oil

Separate the Chinese leaves and pak choi and wash well. Cut into 2.5 cm/1 inch strips. Separate the broccoli into small florets. Heat a wok or large frying pan, add the sesame seeds and stir-fry for 30 seconds or until browned.

Add the oil to the wok and when hot, add the ginger, garlic and chillies and stir-fry for 30 seconds. Add the broccoli and stir-fry for 1 minute. Add the Chinese leaves and pak choi and stir-fry for a further 1 minute.

Pour the chicken stock and Chinese rice wine into the wok with the soy and black bean sauces. Season to taste with pepper and add the sugar. Reduce the heat and simmer for 6–8 minutes, or until the vegetables are tender but still firm to the bite. Tip into a warmed serving dish, removing the chillies if preferred. Drizzle with the sesame oil and serve immediately.

*Try this:* FOR AN ALTERNATIVE: 318   FOR A LIGHT BITE: 34

# Prawn Special Fried Rice

**SERVES 4**

225 g/8 oz raw prawns,
   peeled
2 tbsp light soy sauce
1 tsp caster sugar
2.5 cm/1 inch piece fresh
   root ginger, peeled
   and grated

4 medium eggs
pinch of salt
1 tbsp freshly chopped
   coriander
2 tbsp freshly chopped
   parsley
3 tbsp sunflower oil

1 bunch spring onions,
   trimmed and finely sliced
350 g/12 oz cooked
   long-grain rice
50 g/2 oz frozen peas,
   thawed
freshly ground black pepper

Using a small, sharp knife, remove the thin black thread that runs down the back of the prawns, then rinse and pat dry with absorbent kitchen paper. Chop in half or thirds, then place in a bowl with the soy sauce, sugar and ginger. Mix well and reserve.

Whisk together 2 of the eggs with salt and the chopped coriander and parsley. Heat 1 tablespoon of the oil in a wok over a low heat and pour in the egg mixture. Tilt the wok so the mixture spreads to an even layer.

Cook gently, stirring, until the mixture begins to set, then stop stirring and cook for a further 30 seconds until the underneath is golden brown and the top is still slightly creamy. Tip the omelette onto a clean chopping board and leave to cool. When cold, roll up loosely and cut into fine slices. Wipe the wok clean.

Heat the remaining oil and stir-fry the prawns for 2–3 minutes, or until they are cooked and have turned pink. Add the spring onions and continue stir-frying for a further 1–2 minutes.

Add the rice and peas and stir-fry for 2 minutes. Lightly beat the remaining 2 eggs. Drizzle over the rice, then stir-fry for about 30 seconds until scrambled. Serve immediately, sprinkled with the shredded omelette.

# Coconut Sorbet
# with Mango Sauce

**SERVES 4**

2 sheets gelatine
250 g/9 oz caster sugar
600 ml/1 pint coconut milk

2 mangos, peeled, pitted
and sliced
2 tbsp icing sugar

zest and juice of 1 lime

Set the freezer to rapid freeze, 2 hours before freezing the sorbet. Place the sheets of gelatine in a shallow dish, pour over cold water to cover and leave for 15 minutes. Squeeze out excess moisture before use.

Meanwhile, place the caster sugar and 300 ml/½ pint of the coconut milk in a heavy-based saucepan and heat gently, stirring occasionally, until the sugar has dissolved. Remove from the heat.

Add the soaked gelatine to the saucepan and stir gently until dissolved. Stir in the remaining coconut milk. Leave until cold.

Pour the gelatine and coconut mixture into a freezable container and place in the freezer. Leave for at least 1 hour, or until the mixture has started to form ice crystals. Remove and beat with a spoon, then return to the freezer and continue to freeze until the mixture is frozen, beating at least twice more during this time.

Meanwhile, make the sauce. Place the sliced mango, icing sugar and the lime zest and juice in a food processor and blend until smooth. Spoon into a small jug.

Leave the sorbet to soften in the refrigerator for at least 30 minutes before serving. Serve scoops of sorbet on individual plates with a little of the mango sauce poured over. Remember to turn the freezer to normal setting.

 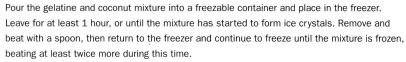 *Try this:* FOR AN ALTERNATIVE: 378 FOR A LIGHT BITE: 258

# Rose–water Doughballs with Yogurt Sauce

**MAKES 30**

300 g/11 oz self-raising
   flour, sifted
50 g/2 oz ground almonds
75 g/3 oz butter, cubed
75 ml/3 fl oz natural yogurt

2 tsp rose water
grated zest of 1 orange
600 ml/1 pint vegetable oil
65 g/2½ oz caster sugar
lime zest, to decorate

**For the yogurt sauce:**
200 ml/7 fl oz natural yogurt
2 tsp rose water
grated zest of 1 lime
1 tbsp icing sugar, sifted

To make the yogurt sauce, blend the yogurt with the rose water, lime zest and sugar in a small bowl. Pour into a serving jug, cover with clingfilm and refrigerate until ready to serve.

Place the flour and ground almonds in a large bowl and, using your fingertips, rub in the butter until the mixture resembles fine breadcrumbs.

Add the yogurt, rose water and orange zest to the crumbed mixture, pour in 50 ml/2 fl oz of warm water and mix with a knife to form a soft pliable dough. Turn on to a lightly floured board and knead for 2 minutes or until smooth, then divide the dough into 30 small balls.

Heat the vegetable oil in a large wok or deep-fat fryer to 190˚C/375˚F, or until a bread cube dropped into the oil sizzles and turns golden brown. Working in batches of a few at a time, deep-fry the dough balls for 5–6 minutes or until golden brown. Using a slotted spoon, remove the balls from the oil and drain on absorbent kitchen paper.

Pour the caster sugar on a plate and roll all the dough balls in the sugar until well coated. Decorate with a little lime zest and serve immediately with the yogurt sauce.

# Chocolate & Lemon Grass Mousse

**SERVES 4**

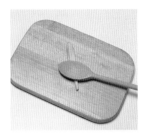

| | | |
|---|---|---|
| 3 lemon grass stalks, outer leaves removed | 150 g/5 oz milk chocolate, broken into small pieces | 150 ml/¼ pint double cream |
| 200 ml/7 fl oz milk | 2 medium egg yolks | juice of 2 lemons |
| 2 sheets gelatine | 50 g/2 oz caster sugar | 1 tbsp caster sugar |
| | | lemon zest, to decorate |

Use a wooden spoon to bruise the lemon grass, then cut in half. Pour the milk into a large heavy-based saucepan, add the lemon grass and bring to the boil. Remove from the heat, leave to infuse for 1 hour, then strain. Place the gelatine in a shallow dish, pour over cold water to cover and leave for 15 minutes. Squeeze out excess moisture before use.

Place the chocolate in a small bowl set over a saucepan of gently simmering water and leave until melted. Make sure the water does not touch the bowl.

Whisk the egg yolks and sugar together until thick, then whisk in the flavoured milk. Pour into a clean saucepan and cook gently, stirring continuously, until the mixture starts to thicken. Remove from the heat, stir in the melted chocolate and gelatine and leave to cool for a few minutes.

Whisk the double cream until soft peaks form, then stir into the cooled milk mixture to form a mousse. Spoon into individual ramekins or moulds and leave in the refrigerator for 2 hours or until set.

Just before serving, pour the lemon juice into a small saucepan, bring to the boil, then simmer for 3 minutes or until reduced. Add the sugar and heat until dissolved, stirring continuously. Serve the mousse drizzled with the lemon sauce and decorated with lemon zest.

# Coconut Rice Served with Stewed Ginger Fruits

**SERVES 6–8**

1 vanilla pod
450 ml/¾ pint coconut milk
1.1 litres/2 pints
semi-skimmed milk
600 ml/1 pint double cream
100 g/3½ oz caster sugar
2 star anise

8 tbsp toasted desiccated
coconut
250 g/9 oz short-grain
pudding rice
1 tsp melted butter
2 mandarin oranges, peeled
and pith removed

1 star fruit, sliced
50 g/2 oz stem ginger,
finely diced
300 ml/½ pint sweet
white wine
caster sugar, to taste

Preheat the oven to 160°C/325°F/Gas Mark 3. Using a sharp knife, split the vanilla pod in half lengthways, scrape out the seeds from the pods and place both the pod and seeds in a large heavy-based casserole dish. Pour in the coconut milk, the semi-skimmed milk and the double cream and stir in the sugar, star anise and 4 tablespoons of the toasted coconut. Bring to the boil, then simmer for 10 minutes, stirring occasionally. Remove the vanilla pod and star anise.

Wash the rice and add to the milk. Simmer gently for 25–30 minutes or until the rice is tender, stirring frequently. Stir in the melted butter.

Divide the mandarins into segments and place in a saucepan with the sliced star fruit and stem ginger. Pour in the white wine and 300 ml/½ pint water, bring to the boil, then reduce the heat and simmer for 20 minutes or until the liquid has reduced and the fruits softened. Add sugar to taste.

Serve the rice, topped with the stewed fruits and the remaining toasted coconut.

*Try this:* FOR AN ALTERNATIVE: 372  FOR A LIGHT BITE: 114

# Hot Cherry Fritters

**SERVES 6**

50 g/2 oz butter
pinch of salt
2 tbsp caster sugar
125 g/4 oz plain flour, sifted
¼ tsp ground cinnamon

25 g/1 oz ground almonds
3 medium eggs, lightly
   beaten
175 g/6 oz cherries, stoned
sunflower oil for frying

2 tbsp icing sugar
1 tsp cocoa powder
sprigs of fresh mint,
   to decorate

Place the butter, salt and sugar in a small saucepan with 225 ml/8 fl oz water. Heat gently until the butter has melted, then add the flour and ground cinnamon and beat over a low heat until the mixture leaves the sides of the pan.

Remove the saucepan from the heat and beat in the ground almonds. Gradually add the eggs, beating well after each addition. Finally stir in the cherries.

Pour 5 cm/2 inches depth of oil in a wok and heat until it reaches 180°C/350°F on a sugar thermometer. Drop in heaped teaspoons of the mixture, cooking 4 or 5 at a time for about 2 minutes, or until lightly browned and crisp.

Remove the fritters from the pan with a slotted spoon and drain on absorbent kitchen paper. Keep warm in a low oven while cooking the remaining fritters. Arrange on a warmed serving plate and dust with the icing sugar and cocoa powder. Decorate with mint sprigs and serve hot.

*Try this:* FOR AN ALTERNATIVE: 374   FOR A LIGHT BITE: 324

# Index

**B**

Baked Thai Chicken Wings 226
Barbecued Pork Fillet 174
Barbecue Pork Steamed Buns 70
Bean & Cashew Stir Fry 328
Beef
Chilli Beef 156
Coconut Beef 148
Fried Rice with Chilli Beef 198
Shredded Beef in Hoisin Sauce 200
Spicy Beef Pancakes 42
Stir-fried Beef with Vermouth 192
Sweet-&-Sour Shredded Beef 342
Szechuan Beef 170
Beef & Baby Corn Stir Fry 164
Beef Curry with Lemon & Arborio Rice 202
Beef Noodle Soup 294
Beef with Paprika 196
Braised Chicken with Aubergine 210

**C**

Cashew & Pork Stir Fry 172
Cantonese Chicken Wings 50
Char Sui Pork & Noodle Salad 284
Chicken
Baked Thai Chicken Wings 226
Braised Chicken with Aubergine 210
Cantonese Chicken Wings 50
Chinese Braised White Chicken with Three
Sauces 222
Clear Chicken & Mushroom Soup 20
Creamy Chicken & Tofu Soup 22
Green Chicken Curry 246
Orange Roasted Whole Chicken 224
Red Chicken Curry 232

Soy-glazed Chicken Thighs 78
Steamed, Crispy, Citrus Chicken 274
Stir-fried Lemon Chicken 214
Szechuan Sesame Chicken 348
Thai Chicken Fried Rice 242
Thai Chicken with Chilli & Peanuts 236
Thai Coconut Chicken 258
Chicken & Baby Vegetable Stir Fry 254
Chicken & Cashew Nuts 262
Chicken & Lamb Satay 346
Chicken Chow Mein 248
Chicken-filled Spring Rolls 72
Chicken in Black Bean Sauce 244
Chicken Noodle Soup 296
Chicken Satay Salad 250
Chicken with Noodles 290
Chilli Beef 156
Chilli Lamb 188
Chinese Barbecue-style Quails with Aubergines 220
Chinese Bean Sauce Noodles 292
Chinese Braised White Chicken with Three Sauces 222
Chinese Egg Fried Rice 310
Chinese Five Spice Marinated Salmon 118
Chinese Fried Rice 304
Chinese-glazed Poussin with Green & Black Rice 208
Chinese Leaf & Mushroom Soup 64
Chinese Leaves with Sweet-&-Sour Sauce 326
Chinese Omelette 334
Chinese Steamed Sea Bass with Black Beans 108
Chocolate & Lemon Grass Mousse 376
Clear Chicken & Mushroom Soup 20
Coconut Beef 148
Coconut Rice Served with Stewed Ginger Fruits 378
Coconut Seafood 124
Coconut Sorbet with Mango Sauce 372
Cooked Vegetable Salad with Satay Sauce 316

Corn Fritters with Hot & Spicy Relish 324
Crab
Deep-fried Crab Wontons 104
Sweetcorn & Crab Soup 60
Thai Coconut Crab Curry 98
Thai Crab Cakes 36
Creamy Chicken & Tofu Soup 22
Creamy Spicy Shellfish 138
Crispy Aromatic Duck 352
Crispy Noodle Salad 298
Crispy Pancake Rolls 336
Crispy Pork with Tangy Sauce 180
Crispy Prawn Stir Fry 134
Crispy Prawns with Chinese Dipping Sauce 54
Crispy Pork Wontons 30
Crispy Roast Duck Legs with Pancakes 218

**D**

Deep-fried Crab Wontons 104
Dim Sum Pork Parcels 356
Duck
Crispy Aromatic Duck 352
Crispy Roast Duck Legs with Pancakes 218
Hoisin Duck & Greens Stir Fry 268
Honey-glazed Duck in Kumquat Sauce 354
Hot-&-Sour Duck 240
Seared Duck with Pickled Plums 228
Shredded Duck in Lettuce Leaves 80
Stir-fried Duck with Cashews 212
Teriyaki Duck with Plum Chutney 272
Duck & Exotic Fruit Stir Fry 270
Duck in Black Bean Sauce 206
Duck in Crispy Wonton Shells 252

**F**

Fish

Fried Fish with Thai Chilli Dipping Sauce 92
Poached Fish Dumplings with Creamy Chilli
    Sauce 56
Sweet-&-Sour Battered Fish 40
Sweet-&-Sour Fish 110
see also; cod; crab; monkfish; prawns; salmon;
    scallops; shellfish; squid; swordfish
Fish Balls in Hot Yellow Bean Sauce 112
Fragrant Thai Swordfish with Peppers 96
Fried Fish with Thai Chilli Dipping Sauce 92
Fried Rice with Bamboo Shoots & Ginger 330
Fried Rice with Chilli Beef 198

**G**
Ginger Lobster 362
Green Chicken Curry 246
Green Turkey Curry 234

**H**
Hoisin Duck & Greens Stir Fry 268
Hoisin Pork 146
Honey-glazed Duck in Kumquat Sauce 354
Honey Pork with Rice Noodles & Cashews 184
Hot-&-Sour Duck 240
Hot-&-Sour Soup 62
Hot-&-Sour Squid 46
Hot Cherry Fritters 380

**K**
Kung-pao Lamb 344

**L**
Lamb
    Chicken & Lamb Satay 346
    Chilli Lamb 188
    Kung-pao Lamb 344
    Spicy Lamb & Peppers 176
Laksa Malayan Rice Noodle Soup 66
Lamb with Stir-fried Vegetables 168
Lime & Sesame Turkey 266
Lion's Head Pork Balls 44

Lobster
    Ginger Lobster 362
    Warm Lobster Salad with Hot Thai Dressing 102
Lobster & Prawn Curry 126

**M**
Mixed Satay Sticks 32
Mixed Vegetables Stir Fry 318
Monkfish
    Steamed Monkfish with Chilli & Ginger 84
Moo Shi Pork 28
Mussels
    Thai Green Fragrant Mussels 360

**N**
Noodles
    Chicken with Noodles 290
    Chinese Bean Sauce Noodles 292
    Honey Pork with Rice Noodles & Cashews 184
    Pork Fried Noodles 144
    Singapore Noodles 280
    Szechuan Turkey Noodles 264
    Thai Spring Rolls with Noodles & Dipping Sauce 278
    Vegetables in Coconut Milk with Rice Noodles 338
    Wonton Noodle Soup 24
Noodles with Turkey & Mushrooms 260

**O**
Orange Roasted Whole Chicken 224
Oriental Noodle & Peanut Salad with Coriander 282
Oriental Spicy Scallops 132

**P**
Poached Fish Dumplings with Creamy Chilli Sauce 56
Pork
    Barbecued Pork Fillet 174
    Barbecue Pork Steamed Buns 70
    Cashew & Pork Stir Fry 172
    Char Sui Pork & Noodle Salad 284
    Crispy Pork with Tangy Sauce 180
    Crispy Pork Wontons 30

Dim Sum Pork Parcels 356
Hoisin Pork 146
Honey Pork with Rice Noodles & Cashews 184
Lion's Head Pork Balls 44
Moo Shi Pork 28
Speedy Pork with Yellow Bean Sauce 182
Spicy Pork 152
Sweet-&-Sour Pork 186
Pork Cabbage Parcels 178
Pork Fried Noodles 144
Pork in Peanut Sauce 190
Pork Meatballs with Vegetables 150
Pork Spring Rolls 160
Pork with Black Bean Sauce 158
Pork with Spring Vegetables & Sweet Chilli Sauce 194
Pork with Tofu 358
Pork with Tofu & Coconut 154
Prawns
    Crispy Prawn Stir Fry 134
    Crispy Prawns with Chinese Dipping Sauce 54
    Lobster & Prawn Curry 126
    Red Prawn Curry with Jasmine-scented Rice 86
    Scallops & Prawns Braised in Lemon Grass 94
    Sesame Prawns 68
    Sesame Prawn Toasts 38
    Spicy Prawns in Lettuce Cups 48
    Stir-fried Tiger Prawns 122
    Szechuan Chilli Prawns 106
    Thai Fried Rice with Prawns & Chillies 288
    Thai Hot-&-Sour Prawn Soup 58
    Thai Marinated Prawns 100
    Thai Prawn & Rice Noodle Salad 88
    Thai Spicy Prawn & Lettuce Noodle Soup 300
    Sour & Spicy Prawn Soup 364
Prawn Fried Rice 128
Prawn Salad with Toasted Rice 74
Prawn Special Fried Rice 370

**R**
Red Chicken Curry 232
Red Prawn Curry with Jasmine-scented Rice 86

Rice
  Beef Curry with Lemon & Arborio Rice 202
  Chinese Egg Fried Rice 310
  Chinese-glazed Poussin with Green & Black Rice 208
  Chinese Fried Rice 304
  Coconut Rice Served with Stewed Ginger Fruits 378
  Fried Rice with Bamboo Shoots & Ginger 330
  Fried Rice with Chilli Beef 198
  Prawn Fried Rice 128
  Prawn Salad with Toasted Rice 74
  Red Prawn Curry with Jasmine-scented Rice 86
  Royal Fried Rice 366
  Special Fried Rice 162
  Spicy Cod Rice 136
  Thai Chicken Fried Rice 242
  Thai Fried Rice with Prawns & Chillies 288
  Thai Rice Cakes with Mango Salsa 286
Rose-water Doughballs with Yogurt Sauce 374
Royal Fried Rice 366

S
Salmon
  Chinese Five Spice Marinated Salmon 118
  Teriyaki Salmon 130
Savoury Wontons 322
Scallops
  Oriental Spicy Scallops 132
Scallops & Prawns Braised in Lemon Grass 94
Scallops with Black Bean Sauce 120
Seafood Noodle Salad 302
Seared Duck with Pickled Plums 228
Sesame Prawns 68
Sesame Prawn Toasts 38
Shellfish, Creamy Spicy Shellfish 138
Shredded Beef in Hoisin Sauce 200
Shredded Duck in Lettuce Leaves 80
Singapore Noodles 280
Sour & Spicy Prawn Soup 364
Soy-glazed Chicken Thighs 78

Special Fried Rice 162
Speedy Pork with Yellow Bean Sauce 182
Spicy Beef Pancakes 42
Spicy Cod Rice 136
Spicy Lamb & Peppers 176
Spicy Pork 152
Spicy Prawns in Lettuce Cups 48
Squid
  Hot-&-Sour Squid 46
  Stir-fried Squid with Asparagus 116
Steamed, Crispy, Citrus Chicken 274
Steamed Monkfish with Chilli & Ginger 84
Steamed Whole Trout with Ginger & Spring Onion 114
Sticky Braised Spare Ribs 76
Stir-fried Beef with Vermouth 192
Stir-fried Duck with Cashews 212
Stir-fried Greens 368
Stir-fried Lemon Chicken 214
Stir-fried Squid with Asparagus 116
Stir-fried Tiger Prawns 122
Sweet-&-Sour Battered Fish 40
Sweet-&-Sour Fish 110
Sweet-&-Sour Pork 186
Sweet-&-Sour Shredded Beef 342
Sweet-&-Sour Spareribs 166
Sweet-&-Sour Turkey 256
Sweetcorn & Crab Soup 60
Sweetcorn Fritters 34
Szechuan Beef 170
Szechuan Chilli Prawns 106
Szechuan Sesame Chicken 348
Szechuan Turkey Noodles 264

T
Tempura 140
Teriyaki Duck with Plum Chutney 272
Teriyaki Salmon 130
Thai Chicken Fried Rice 242
Thai Chicken with Chilli & Peanuts 236
Thai Coconut Chicken 258
Thai Coconut Crab Curry 98

Thai Crab Cakes 36
Thai Curried Seafood 90
Thai Curry with Tofu 332
Thai Fried Rice with Prawns & Chillies 288
Thai Green Fragrant Mussels 360
Thai Hot-&-Sour Prawn Soup 58
Thai Marinated Prawns 100
Thai Prawn & Rice Noodle Salad 88
Thai Rice Cakes with Mango Salsa 286
Thai Shellfish Soup 26
Thai Spicy Prawn & Lettuce Noodle Soup 300
Thai Spring Rolls with Noodles & Dipping Sauce 278
Thai Stir-fried Spicy Turkey 238
Thai Stuffed Eggs with Spinach & Sesame Seeds 320
Thai Stuffed Omelette 230
Thai-style Cauliflower & Potato Curry 314
Tofu
  Creamy Chicken & Tofu Soup 22
  Pork with Tofu 358
  Pork with Tofu & Coconut 154
  Thai Curry with Tofu 332
Turkey
  Green Turkey Curry 234
  Lime & Sesame Turkey 266
  Noodles with Turkey & Mushrooms 260
  Sweet-&-Sour Turkey 256
  Szechuan Turkey Noodles 264
  Thai Stir-fried Spicy Turkey 238
Turkey & Vegetable Stir Fry 216
Turkey with Oriental Mushrooms 350

V
Vegetables in Coconut Milk with Rice Noodles 338
Vegetable Tempura 312
Vegetable Thai Spring Rolls 52

W
Warm Lobster Salad with Hot Thai Dressing 102
Warm Noodle Salad with Sesame & Peanut Dressing 308
Wonton Noodle Soup 24